Prepare for the Great Tribulation and the Era of Peace

Prepare for the Great Tribulation and the Era of Peace

Volume V:
October 1, 1996 – December 31, 1996

by John Leary

Queenship
PUBLISHING COMPANY
P.O Box 42028 Santa Barbara, CA 93140-2028
(800) 647-9882 • (805) 957-4893 • Fax: (805) 957-1631

The publisher recognizes and accepts that the final authority regarding these apparitions and messages rests with the Holy See of Rome, to whose judgement we willingly submit.

– The Publisher

Cover art by Josyp Terelya

©1997 Queenship Publishing

Library of Congress Number # 96-68181

Published by:
Queenship Publishing
P.O. Box 42028
Santa Barbara, CA 93140-2028
(800) 647-9882 • (805) 957-4893 • Fax: (805) 957-1631

Printed in the United States of America

ISBN: 1-882972-97-X

Acknowledgments

It is in a spirit of deep gratitude that I would like to acknowledge first the Holy Trinity: Father, Jesus, and the Holy Spirit, the Blessed Virgin Mary and the many saints and angels who have made this book possible.

My wife, Carol, has been an invaluable partner. Her complete support of faith and prayers has allowed us to work as a team. This was especially true in the many hours of indexing and proofing of the manuscript. All of our family has been a source of care and support.

I am greatly indebted to Josyp Terelya for his very gracious offer to provide the art work for this publication. He has spent three months of work and prayer to provide us with a selection of many original pictures. He wanted very much to enhance the visions and messages with these beautiful and provocative works. You will experience some of them throughout these volumes.

A very special thank you goes to my spiritual director, Fr. Leo J. Klem, C.S.B. No matter what hour I called him, he was always there with his confident wisdom, guidance and discernment. His love, humility, deep faith and trust are a true inspiration.

My appreciation also goes to Father John V. Rosse, my good pastor at Holy Name of Jesus Church. He has been open, loving and supportive from the very beginning.

There are many friends and relatives whose interest, love and prayerful support have been a real gift from God. Our own Wednesday, Monday and First Saturday prayer groups deserve a special thank you for their loyalty and faithfulness.

Finally, I would like to thank Bob and Claire Schaefer of Queenship Publishing and their spiritual director, Fr. Luke Zimmer for providing the opportunity to bring this message of preparation, love and warnings to you the people of God.

John Leary, Jr.
January 1996

Dedication

To the Most Holy Trinity

God

The Father, Son and Holy Spirit

The Source of

All

Life, Love and Wisdom

Publisher's Foreword

John has, with some exceptions, been having visions twice a day since they began in July, 1993. The first vision of the day usually takes place during morning Mass, immediately after he receives the Eucharist. If the name of the church is not mentioned, it is a local Rochester, NY, church. When out of town, the church name is included in the text. The second vision occurs in the evening, either at Perpetual Adoration or at the prayer group that is held at John's.

Various names appear in the text. Most of the time, the names appear only once or twice. Their identity is not important to the message and their reason for being in the text is evident. First names have been used, when requested by the individual. The name Maria E., which occurs quite often, is the visionary Maria Esperanza Bianchini of Betania, Venezuela.

We are grateful to Josep Terelya for the cover art, as well as for the art throughout the book. Josyp is a well-known visionary and also, the author of *Witness* and most recently *In the Kingdom of the Spirit.*

This volume covers visions from October 1, 1996 through December 31, 1996. The volumes will now be coming out quarterly due to the urgency of the messages. Volume I contains visions from July, 1993 through June, 1994. Volume II contains visions from July, 1994 through June, 1995. Volume III contains visions from July, 1995 through July 10, 1996. Volume IV contains visions from July, 11 1996 through September 30, 1996.

The Publisher
January, 1997

Foreword

It was in July of 1993 that Almighty God, especially through Jesus, His Eternal Word, entered the life of John Leary in a most remarkable way. John is 54 years old and works as a chemist at Eastman Kodak Co., Rochester, New York. He lives in a modest house in the suburbs of Rochester with Carol, his wife of thirty-one years, and Catherine, his youngest daughter. His other two daughters, Jeanette and Donna, are married and have homes of their own. John has been going to daily Mass since he was seventeen and has been conducting a weekly prayer group in his own home for twenty-four years. For a long time, he has been saying fifteen decades of the Rosary each day.

In April of 1993 he and his wife made a pilgrimage to Our Lady's shrine in Medjugorje, Yugoslavia. While there, he felt a special attraction to Jesus in the Blessed Sacrament. There he became aware that the Lord Jesus was asking him to change his way of life and to make Him his first priority. A month later in his home, Our Lord spoke to him and asked if he would give over his will to Him to bring about a very special mission. Without knowing clearly to what he was consenting, John, strong in faith and trust, agreed to all the Lord would ask.

On July 21, 1993 the Lord gave him an inkling of what would be involved in this new calling. He was returning home from Toronto in Canada where he had listened to a talk of Maria Esperanza (a visionary from Betania, Venezuela) and had visited Josyp Terelya. While in bed, he had a mysterious interior vision of a newspaper headline that spelled "DISASTER." Thus began a series of daily and often twice daily interior visions along with messages, mostly from Jesus. Other messages were from God the Father, the Holy Spirit, the Blessed Virgin Mary, his guardian angel and many of the saints, especially St. Therese of Lisieux. These messages he recorded on his word processor. In the beginning, they were quite short, but they became more extensive as the weeks passed by. At the time of this writing, he is still receiving visions and messages.

These daily spiritual experiences, which occur most often immediately following Communion, consist of a brief vision which becomes the basis of the message that follows. They range widely on a great variety of subjects, but one might group them under the following categories: warnings, teachings and love messages. Occasionally, there are personal confirmations of some special requests that he made to the Lord.

The interior visions contain an amazing number of different pictures, some quite startling, which hardly repeat themselves. In regard to the explicit messages that are inspired by each vision, they contain deep insights into the kind of relationship God wishes to establish with His human creatures. There, also, is an awareness of how much He loves us and yearns for our response. As a great saint once wrote: "Love is repaid only by love." On the other hand, God is not a fool to be treated lightly. In fact, did not Jesus once say something about not casting pearls before the swine? Thus, there are certain warnings addressed to those who shrug God off as if He did not exist or is not important in human life.

Along with such warnings, we become more conscious of the reality of Satan and the forces of evil "...which wander through the world seeking the ruin of souls." We used to recite this at the end of each low Mass. In His love and concern for us, Our Lord keeps constantly pointing out how frail we humans are in the face of such evil angelic powers. God is speaking of the necessity of daily prayer, of personal penance, and of turning away from atheistic and material enticements which are so much a part of our modern environment.

Perhaps the most controversial parts of the messages are those which deal with what we commonly call Apocalyptic. Unusual as these may be, in my judgment, they are not basically any different than what we find in the last book of the New Testament or in some of the writings of St. Paul. After a careful and prayerful reading of the hundreds of pages in this book, I have not found anything contrary to the authentic teaching authority of the Roman Catholic Church.

The 16th Century Spanish mystic, St. John of the Cross, gives us sound guidelines for discerning the authenticity of this sort of phenomenon involving visions, locutions, etc. According to him, there are three possible sources: the devil, some kind of self-imposed hypnosis or God. I have been John's spiritual confidant for over three years. I have tested him in various spiritual ways and I am most confident that all he has put into these messages is neither of the devil nor of some kind of mental illness. Rather, they are from the God who, in His love for us, wishes to reveal His own Divine mind and heart. He has used John for this. I know that John is quite ready to abide by any decision of proper ecclesiastical authority on what he has written in this book

Rev. Leo J. Klem, C.S.B.
January 4, 1996
Rochester, New York

Visions and Messages
of John Leary:

Tuesday, October 1, 1996: (St. Therese of Lisieux)

After Communion, I could see St. Therese in her brown habit and she said: *"My dear son, John, I am happy to see you on my feast day. It is a pleasure to come and talk to you, my son. You must pray in all you do that Jesus will work through you. He is the one you must follow and be in conformance with his will. You know how much I seek out souls for Jesus, and I relish in the work you are doing. God has touched you in a special way as His instrument. Guard yourself against the evil one, for he is always lurking to do you harm. With the power of Jesus on your side, beckon for His help at all times, so you may remain open to His service. I close now as I ask you to remember me, and to call on my help when you need me. Thank you."*

Later, I could see again the scene I had just viewed as I came into the chapel. A wind was blowing dust around and it blew an empty box about which represented my books. Jesus said: *"My son, many will have the opportunity to preview the coming events through the messages and visions in your books. Some will read them out of curiosity, while others will take it seriously. I have told you that I will use My words to touch those hearts open to My love. Even those, who reject these messages, will have to deal with the messages as they come to fruition. It is important to continue your updates to keep the people informed of events as they occur. In your vision you are seeing the wind buffeting the box, indicating how you will meet some opposition to these messages. Some will not believe and resent someone trying to scare the people. As time approaches the tribulation, you will even be persecuted for fighting the Antichrist's plans. Evil men will try to remove the books, and keep them from being printed or distributed. Go and witness My Word as much as possible now, for there will come a time when you will not be allowed to talk. These messages are important to be spread, since they offer a message of hope even in the face of an evil age. Rejoice, My people, for soon all of your trials will come to an end with My victory over Satan."*

Wednesday, October 2, 1996: (Guardian Angel Day)
After Communion, I requested a visit from Mark, my guardian angel, through Jesus. Mark said: *"My dear little one, you can request my messages at anytime, not just today. Just as I stand before Jesus, He has informed you that as these evil days increase, we will be able to use our powers more in the battle against the demons. I will be watching out for you even when you must deal with demon attacks. It is wise to bring others with you when you request help in healing either physically or spiritually. In addition to their help, you can actually gain help from other's angels as well. Angels play an important role in people's protection. You do not even realize how much we help you everyday. Give thanks to God and me for all the angels do for man. Call on us in your need as well."*

Thursday, October 3, 1996:
After Communion, I could see two disciples dressed in flowing robes. Jesus said: *"My faithful, I send My disciples and messengers out today in pairs as I did when I was on the earth. This again is a time of harvest, but for souls and not just crops. This is why the harvest master needs contrite souls willing to do My work of spreading the Gospel message. Prepare My people for this great purification of the earth. The battle for souls is being waged right now. Those in My hearing should heed this warning of preparation. Seek My sacrament of reconciliation to forgive your sins and make a clean home for Me to rest in. Those souls who do not listen and refuse to repent will be thrown on the fire to burn with the refuse of the harvest. Choose Me and you choose life everlasting."*

Later, at the prayer group, I could see Mary come dressed in white with beams of light surrounding her. Mary said: *"My dear children, I come to celebrate my month of October and my Feast of the Holy Rosary. I am happy to receive your Rosaries for my intentions. I encourage all of you to pray the daily Rosary. Even more beautiful would be to pray the Rosary together as a family. Those families are blessed who pray together. My Rosary is your weapon against Satan — use it often to protect yourself from his temptations."* I could see the barriers and walls as in the Mid-East. Jesus said: *"My people, I ask you to pray for My peace in the Holy Lands where there is much unrest. Unless these people strive for peace, they will find only wars and killings. Without peace in their hearts and a willingness to compromise their differences, you will see a widening conflict over this land."* I could see some people wearing special glasses to see in the dark. Jesus said: *"My people, beware of those agents during the tribulation who will be spying on your every movement. Various electronic devices will be used to know everyone's whereabouts. Those under My protection need not fear these people, since I will guard you while you are at My refuges or in hiding."* I could see several large stairways that led up to a line of train cars. I could see many people climbing the stairs into the trains under guard as they were being taken to detention centers. Jesus said: *"My people, I have warned you to pray that My angels lead you to safety in hiding or to My refuges. Those, who do not go and are deemed enemies of the Antichrist, will be sent on trains and trucks to the nearest detention centers. There, many will suffer persecution and a bare living."* I could see some empty fields and there were no crops being grown. Jesus said: *"My people, for years you have paid farmers not to grow crops, and have failed to help those countries sufficiently in their hunger. You, yourselves, will soon see hard times, since you have squandered opportunities to help others for the sake of money and your prices. Be willing to share what you have, or what little you have, will be taken away from you."* I could see Jesus before me and I was praying that He send us a love message. Jesus said: *"My son, I realize your plight in these times of trial. I truly love all of My people with an infinite unconditional love. I love even those who refuse Me or ignore Me. It is you, My people, that limit the extent of your love for Me. I promise you eternal life through the love I have for you when I died on the cross for you. Come to Me all those seeking rest and I will comfort you. Put your trust in My help each day and I will guide you. All of*

My graces are here for all those who ask Me. Acknowledge Me before men, and I will acknowledge you before My Father in Heaven." I could see some food prepared on some trays. Jesus said: *"My people, I wish to clarify any confusion on those messages concerning food and the famine. By spreading this message, it is hoped that everyone will help in preparing some food storage. This is not meant to hoard food, but to store it for the day when little will be available. I will help men in this work. Still there will be some abusing this storage to have control over people. Those who work with the Antichrist in restricting the buying and selling of food, will have a severe punishment awaiting them in the judgment. Have no fear and follow My warnings and you will be protected."*

Friday, October 4, 1996:

After Communion, I could see a window of suffering that we all will have to go through in the coming purification. Jesus said: *"My people, as the eve of My purification is upon you, you too will be stripped of your possessions and creature comforts. Job was tested and questioned My plans, but later he relented that My will be done. You, too, may complain that these chastisements are too severe. If you had to purify the earth as My justice demands, you could no more deal with this scope of evil than Job could deal with nature. Trust in Me, therefore, that what I do has an overall saving grace, which man in his weakness cannot fully understand. My Will will be done and My Love will shine forth on the just. The wicked will be brought to suffer for their crimes, as a reign of peace will come over the land."*

Later, I could see some cards in a game of chance. Jesus said: *"My people, do not seek elusive wealth by gambling or taking risks. Instead, pray for discernment of your talents, and fulfill My plan for you by seeking out jobs with your skills. By being what you are in the market place, you will find wages for your family, should you marry. Do not take chances with your faith either. In order to follow Me, you must give your life over to Me, so you can daily nourish and refresh your faith. A garden will not give forth its crops, unless it be weeded and cared for. Faith, also, must be weeded of your sins, and cared for by seeking My help each day. You will see that by seeking Me first and not depending on yourself alone, I will lead you to success by your hands in this world and the spiritual world. So heed My words and seek order in your life through Me. Do not leave anything to chance, or you will find chaos in this world and the next."*

Saturday, October 5, 1996:

After Communion, I could see Jesus' face on what looked like Veronica's veil in a reliquary. Jesus said: *"My people, I am showing you My face, so you will reverence Me and keep My likeness ever before the faithful. It is important to remember Me every day, so you can keep your focus on Me. If I am not a part of your day, your love for Me will grow cold. This is why people keep pictures of their loved ones in special places in their homes. Keep My picture there also, so your family can be united with Me. Another thought to remember is that you are created in My image. You have free will to choose Me or not, but if you refuse Me, it is like denying a part of your body. You are one with Me and I draw all men to realize that they are a part of My human family. I became a man to show you how much I share life with you in your joys and troubles. Never forget your origins in Me and you will not be far from My kingdom."*

Later, I at first saw a modern Church. Then, I saw some beautiful stained glass windows in an older Church. Jesus said: *"My people, I am showing you the conflict in My Church between those who would follow modernism or liberation theology vs. Those who belong to the faithful remnant that follow My pope son. Satan is trying to drive a wedge between My faithful. Some have itching ears who want change for its own sake. Many customs and traditions, that give reverence to My Blessed Sacrament, are being put down since those people do not recognize My Real Presence. Those, who will deny My Presence and do not seek My forgiveness in Confession, are going down the path to perdition. This schism or separation in My Church over many truths of the faith, will cause many to lose their souls to the devil's easy life without suffering or respect for Me. Do not be tempted to follow the wide road to hell with all of its many creature comforts. Instead, follow the narrow road to heaven by carrying your cross in obedience to My Will. Those who follow their own will, will be lost, but those who follow My will, will be saved. Pray for My help and I will lead you to your heavenly home."*

Sunday, October 6, 1996:

After Communion, I could see a triangle representing the Trinity. In the middle of the triangle I could see people moving to a beautiful area. I could see children being carried. In another scene I could see doors to tombs opening and the dead were rising with their bodies. Jesus said: *"My people, I wish to share with you in this vision of the era of peace, and some descriptions of things then. This is an age when all men will experience the time before Adam's sin on a renewed earth. This will be a time when the aging process will cease in your thirties. Older people will be strengthened to look younger, and the children will mature in their thirties. The animals and man will be in perfect harmony, as you will all grow in perfection at that time. You will be able to call on Me and I will answer you at any time. You will be exposed to full knowledge of My universe. You will live to an old age and many will live to the end of this age. You will experience My love and peace, so you will be as heaven on earth. You will see in this age how I intended the world to be without the influence of evil. When you are truly faced with the glory of My Creation, you will choose to please Me in every facet of your life. Time will continue, but there will be no wars, as you will love your neighbor as you love Me. Only My faithful will be brought back to life with glorified bodies. You will have time to adore Me and serve Me every day. You will be giving Me thanks continually that you have been graced to be present in this age. This is a message of hope I am showing you, so that My faithful, who have been purified, will enjoy their reward in My splendor of My Kingdom."*

Later, I could look up from the bottom of an entrance to an old mine. Jesus said: *"My people, many are finding it hard to understand the need for hiding in the caves. Let Me make it clear that you have never witnessed the power of the Antichrist. You have seen possessed people, but never anyone in complete control by Satan. It is for this very reason that you need to be away from the Antichrist's control, that I am having My angels lead you to a safe place in hiding. I would not lead you to such places unless it is for your best interest both physically and spiritually. You will see Me work marvels of protection against these demons and evil men. I will frustrate their plans and protect your souls from evil. You must have faith in My power through constant prayer in order to hold up in this battle of good and evil. The caves will protect you from bad weather and the searching by evil men. Continue to warn My people not to take the mark of the beast and avoid all electronic means of buying and selling during the tribulation. Follow My Will in how I will lead you, and you will find hope in My protection."*

Monday, October 7, 1996: (Our Lady of the Rosary)
After Communion, I could see a large mountain and a joy and peace in a new land. Jesus said: *"My people, you are witnessing a mountaintop experience when I come again in triumph to defeat satan. After My triumph, I will usher in an era of peace that has been promised even in My scriptures. I have told you many wonderful things you will experience in this time that will be free of evil. Do not doubt how My glory will be carried out at this time, but rejoice in My love, as you are brought closer to perfection before your entry into heaven. Those who have died and are resurrected, will have glorified bodies and will live to the end of this era. Those, who are faithful and live through the tribulation, will have their reward also in My era of peace. These will have their bodies rejuvenated and will live long lives. It is only some of these people who may see death before the end of this era. Do not be concerned over the details of how My Will intends things. It is My keeping with scripture and My promises that are more important. Be joyful in My gifts to you and do not doubt over anything I have given you. I give you all reason to be joyful and your thanks should be ever in your prayer."*

Later, I could see Mary come down a stairway into the living room of a family. She was wearing blue and a crown of flowers. Mary said: *"My dear children, receive me into your home, as if I were walking down the stairs into your own living room. I have mentioned before to have your family pray the family rosary, and I repeat this request on my feast day. Even if you can say only one decade together, you will see the graces of my peace that I will bring to your family. Many families are torn apart by petty jealousies and grudges held against each other over sometimes only pride. I ask you to seek each other's forgiveness and settle your differences. By praying my Rosary, you will encourage peace in your family. By sharing my love, you can bring love to each other. It is only by living in peace in your families, that peace will come to all peoples. This is why I am frequently requesting you to pray for peace in your world, so wars may not engulf your nations and let Satan's hand prevail. Pray with me and my Son, and all of your problems will melt away with the graces, that will be poured over you for saying my Rosary."*

Tuesday, October 8, 1996: (Gospel on Martha & Mary)
After Communion, I saw a water wheel and then a tunnel into a cave. Jesus said: *"My people, you have chosen me over the world and you have indeed, chosen the better portion. It is good to show hospitality toward your neighbor, but when I come knocking at the door of your heart, always be ready to welcome Me into your hearts. I send out My love over everyone. I am awaiting your love response in gratitude for all I have given you. Never think you have gained anything on your own. All that you have has been graced to you by My Father. Give thanks to Me for what you have and pray that you will continue to receive My blessings. Those, who are humble and serve Me, I will see to their every need."*

Later, I could see a beach with the waves rolling in. Then, in front of me I could see a golden gyroscope used to find bearings of direction. Jesus said: *"My people, I am showing you this instrument of finding direction, so that you understand all roads must come through Me. You think many times that you can find your way by yourself without anyone else's help. My faithful know the path they should be taking, but many temptations cause you distraction. Understand when My Will is to heal sinners either physically, spiritually, or both, I use many instruments to convey that healing. You are right in praying that My will be done, when praying over people for a healing. Many powerful healings are still going on which man cannot explain with his science. See to it that you pray for a person's spiritual healing before addressing a physical healing. Again call on many hands when you pray for a healing, and continue to give Me all the praise for any miracles and not yourselves. You will see My witness of faith in these healings, when men are sincere in their hearts and have faith in My healing powers."*

Wednesday, October 9, 1996:

After Communion, I could see some men working on an assembly line. Jesus said: *"My people, I wish to tell you how the work of your hands is a blessing. As some come to work, they think of it more as a drudgery and complain of their lot. Instead of complaining, think of your work in a different light. You are blessed that there are good jobs available. Work by your hands can be the life by which you receive your salvation. When you offer up your work to Me each day, it becomes a beautiful gift of prayer to Me. Many are providing good services that the rest of your fellowmen may be served in their need. Think more of your work as the goods that will help someone and you will see the inner beauty of work as a blessing from your hands. Your work also serves to provide your living and a feeling of worth in your society. After pondering these thoughts, now you can see the love that is molded even in your working hours. Have courage, My friends, and give thanks to God for your work."*

Thursday, October 10, 1996:

After Communion, I could see Maria E. as she was receiving some visitors. I then had a vision of crosses as if they were marching past me. Jesus said: *"My people, what you are seeing in vision, is how many of My faithful will be martyred for believing in My Name. The fact that they were marching, shows you that they were being killed by an invisible or foreign army. Satan will be organizing his agents in various places throughout the world. His people have prepared long ago for this takeover at the tribulation. I am asking you, My people, not to fight this evil with arms. Killing will only promote the death culture of Satan. Instead, when you see evil men taking over by force, you are to call on My angels to lead you to safe places. Let My angels go to battle for you. They alone will exact any punishment for these crimes of murder. As it was in previous times gone by, you will be faced with a ruthless persecution led by the evil one. You should know that you are facing principalities and powers of an evil you have yet to experience. Call on My angels for help and they will deliver you from these evil men."* Later, at the prayer group, I could see some children in a school and there was a little black toy train. Jesus said: *"My people, I am showing you the children, so that you will remember to bring them up in the faith. It is your responsibility as parents to see that the faith gets passed on to future generations. Do not trust this responsibility to others to provide this training. You are the ones to reinforce the gospel message in your lives as examples to them. Guard their innocent souls from all the evil influences around them."* I could see food being stored on some shelves in a pantry. Jesus said: *"My people, again I am showing you this message on food so you may remember to prepare both for the famine and the time before the tribulation. Whatever you can put aside does not have to be fancy or expensive. You are the ones responsible for your family, so prepare for their need. There may be a time during the famine when you may not be able to buy food. Then your storage will be a temporary refuge. I will be watching over you, but I ask you to be prudent in your own affairs."* I could see a choir singing. Jesus said: *"My people, during the era of peace, many of you will be singing My praises as the angels give thanks constantly. This is a beautiful way to give Me reverence. So see a wonderful outpouring of faith when you sing religious songs. This is also a sign of joy and love that you share with each other in My Name. You should understand even now that you can sing songs of thanks to Me for all you have received. My son David has given you the beautiful songs to Me in the Psalms."* I could see an outline of a body where someone was killed and the area inside the outline was shaded with a red color. Jesus said: *"My people, I implore you to stop the killing in all of its forms. Many lives are lost to murders, especially in this evil age. Homicides, abortions and wars are rampant among you, since man has lost a sense of how precious each life is. Pray, My children, for peace in your society and among your nations. All forms of anger must subside or you will kill all those around you. Keep focused on Me and pray daily, that your world will wake up to this evil killing, and that men will repent of their sins."* I could see Our Lady dressed in white above the three little children. Mary came and said: *"My dear children, thank you for having my image among you this evening. It is a commemoration of my coming to the children at Fatima on October 13th. My message of prayer is true to you now, as it was in the messages I gave to the children. See my love for my children is ceaseless. As a good mother I will always be watching over you. Do not fear at any time, but call on me and my Son to help you in any of your needs."* I could see some children celebrating at a birthday party. Jesus said: *"My people, when you are celebrating some precious times as birthdays, weddings or such occasions, call on Me and share your faith with others at that time. Do not think to call on Me only in your want to solve your problems, but share also your beautiful times with Me as well. I look over your whole life. Share your joys with Me as well as your sorrows."* I could see a door open to a mosque and some Arabs were around it. Jesus said: *"My people, this door is open, since it is showing you an opportunity to seek peace in the holy lands. I ask all parties involved, and you also, to pray for peace in this land, where fighting has reached a dangerous level. If love does not quiet the anger among these peoples, worse events of destruction may occur. This could even draw in other nations with various allegiances."*

Friday, October 11, 1996:

After Communion, I could see an outline of blue with rays going all around the shape of where a statue or figure should be. It appeared Our Lady was coming, but she was absent from the picture. Mary said: *"My son, this vision, where I am absent, is to signify how many of My children have no love for Me, or are not thinking of Me. Yes, I am coming to give you encouragement and protection on your trip to My shrine in Marmora. This is blessed land, as you know, and I watch over all of My faithful messengers and those pilgrims who come here. As I have told you before, many graces go out to all those pilgrims, who come with love and devotion for Me in their hearts. You may make a suffering to come, but I will reward you for your efforts. Continue My children in praying your Rosaries, and see these trips as an inspiration to put your faith on fire to share with others."*

Later, I could see an electronic circuit board with several dots all over it. It was being raised out of the water where search crews were looking for debris from the TWA flight 800. Jesus said: *"My people, you are seeing a vision of some evidence which will convince some of an explosive device that downed this plane. This information may not be made public, even if known, so that leads on who might have done it, may help find them. It will be an extremely political problem and will be subdued, since it may be dangerous to speculate on who did it. Many are seeking an answer, but even family members of the victims will be frustrated by such appearing inaction. This again is a sign of terrorism, I mentioned earlier which purposely occurred at the time of the Olympics. Many such events may become more commonplace as this chain of events will be leading up to a world takeover by Satan's agents. Pray to Me for strength in these times to bear your personal testing in faith. My purification will come as these evil forces think they will be in full control. Trust in Me that the evil one's reign will be short. My triumph will conquer all evil, as the evil people will be judged and cast into hell along with the demons. I give you hope even amidst adversity, so you will remember My glorious outcome in My victory over Satan."*

Saturday, October 12, 1996:

After Communion, I could see some people seated in an open train as life was going by. Jesus said: *"My people, you are seeing in vision, a portrayal of how people go through life, as on a train to a destination. Life is a pilgrimage and a test, to discover who you are and where you are going. You know through the scriptures that you are a part of My creation, and as such, you are to love, know and serve Me. I have laid out a plan for your life, which each of you must pray to understand. Although life is troublesome at times, I give each of you an angel to watch over you, so you are not left alone as orphans. Each day you are tested, but you can call on My help at any time. Many suffer each day struggling through life and forget to request My help. You may still have to endure trials when you pray, but you will be doing*

*everything in unison with Me, and life will have more meaning.
Your life is one preparation for your death and your opportunity
to come to heaven. When you understand your purpose for being
here, you can direct your life more to My service. Give thanks to
Me for My love and My gifts. Strive to perfect your lives, so you
will be pleasing to Me, and your soul will be made ready for the
next life in heaven."*

Later, at St. Patrick's Church, Corning, N.Y., after Communion, I could see a darkened Church without any lights. Jesus said:
*"My people, I am always present in your tabernacles which brings
life to your churches. You are seeing the darkness, because in
many hearts, the faith is weak. Those, who give Me lip service on
Sunday, are the same ones who fail to live their faith the rest of
the week. I am asking you, My faithful, to put a light of My love
in your soul and nurture that love in all that you do. You must
realize, that if you read My Word, you should put it into practice,
or you are not listening with true ears of faith. Live each day
following My ways and you will find a joy in serving Me and
your neighbor. Once you become a beacon of true faith by living
what you preach, then others will profit from your example. It is
the light of love that you can share, that will bring back a true
light in the darkness that you have seen. Help your friends to see
how this love of Me should burn freely in all hearts. This taking
away of your control over life is how you will gain in perfection
by living in My Divine Will. See this light of love, My people, and
yearn for it daily."*

Sunday, October 13, 1996:
At Marmora, at the 10th Station (Jesus is Stripped.), I could
see Mary come and she was dressed in a white wedding dress as a
bride. Mary said: *"My dear children, I invite you to this wedding
feast, since it is the joining of my heart with my Son's Heart. You
also, are part of my Son's Body, where you are the bride and He
is your spouse. I bring you to my Son in all that you do. As you
view this station, my Son is asking you to strip yourself of all
worldly cares and possessions. You must place my Son first in
your life and let Him lead you. Give your will over to following
His ways and you will be on the road to your perfection. I ask*

you, my children, to show your love and respect for Him, so that you may understand why He leads you in carrying your own cross. You must suffer in this life, but offer it up to my Son and He will use it for your salvation. Pray your Rosary daily and be ever attentive to my Son's words and His commands."

Later, I could see a huge dark cloud circling overhead and it covered the entire sky. There was a sense that this represented the coming warning. Jesus said: *"My people, you are seeing a sign of my warning which is coming soon. I am coming again to prepare My people spiritually for this event. Remember, I have told you that those with serious sin will suffer a more traumatic experience. I come, therefore, to seek your forgiveness of sin in confession. See that My Sacrament of Reconciliation is your only hope to right yourself with Me before this mini-judgment. I am always here, patiently waiting for your return. If you are sorry for your sins, that is all that I am seeking. This is the beginning of the renewal of your love for Me. Come to Me, My faithful, and I will give you the rest and peace you seek in My graces. Do not try to go through life alone, or you will be lost in your self-pride. See that you need My help and take that first step forward in faith toward your salvation. All those, who come to Me, have nothing to fear. See the folly in your ways and join Me in your daily battles, and I will see to your needs."*

Monday, October 14, 1996: (St. Callistus I)

After Communion, I could see a brick wall and then some slots in the catacombs where the bodies were placed in underground tunnels. Jesus said: *"My people, just as Jonah was in the belly of the fish for three days and I was buried for three days, you too, will have to spend your days in seclusion before My triumph. You will have a hard life during the tribulation of three and a half years, but I will send My angels to protect you from harm. I will feed you and strengthen you for the day of My victory, when you will emerge into the light of My glory. Have faith in Me, My children, and you will have a joy in My era of peace that will have been worth all of your suffering."*

Later, I could see a red brick Church sitting on a hill. Jesus said: *"My people, I am showing you how I will lead My Church in the time of the trial. I am asking My messengers to prepare the people, so they are ready to endure this suffering. Even though I will provide food and shelter for you, it is the fortunate ones who will be in hiding. Those in the detention centers will suffer many abuses and will even be tortured or martyred. You will suffer much in this time, but you need to purify yourselves almost as an earthly purgatory. All of your comforts will be taken away and you will have to endure some mundane hardships. If you did not suffer as I did, how could you be worthy of the gift of life in the era of peace? What else could you offer Me in return for this joy? This trial will have a redeeming grace for you, so do not complain of any problems you must face. Pray, My children, and ready yourselves with My help, for this test of the demons. My angels will be guarding you. Seek My help and I will answer your prayer."*

Tuesday, October 15, 1996: (St. Teresa of Avila)

After Communion, I could see a woman come dressed in a Carmelite habit. St. Teresa said: *"My son, I come to help you get back to your original contemplative plans. Because of your mission, you must be strong in fighting the devil's temptations, which will be coming stronger as your books are saving souls. See to it that you take less interest in sports and the news. Be more concentrated on spending time in prayer, since you need that more now for your public mission. By keeping close to Jesus, you will have a more reserved and joyful spirit in Jesus. These are your goals and you should make them more a part of your life. Be strong in your interior prayer life and the devil cannot influence you."*

Later, I could see a cardinal with a black robe and red fringe. Jesus said: *"My people, you are seeing men in the Church who would like to take over the papacy, and lead the faithful their own way. They will seize on any opportunity, such as the Pope's health or his age. Satan is directing their ambitions and will use them to mislead the people. When you see their pronouncements in conflict with My revealed Scripture, you will see how this is an evil lot that strives for power on an earthly plane. I will gift you with discernment to see how evil these people really are. This new pope, who will replace Pope John Paul II, will be deceptive and lead the people as a tyrant. He will be trying to use his office to promote the Antichrist. Once, you recognize the evil in him, you will remember My words, how he will utter all abominations and blasphemies. Be watchful, for soon you will see his election in violation of the proper succession of popes. This impostor is not to be obeyed, but reject him, since he will be in league with the Antichrist. Pray for My help to discern and avoid these evil men. When this impostor pope comes on the scene, it is another sign to go into hiding."*

Wednesday, October 16, 1996:
After Communion, I could see a dove coming down on the earth. The earth was portrayed with much dust in the air and a chaotic flurry of activity, mostly evil. The Holy Spirit said: *"I am the Spirit of love and I am making my presence known, as I prepare today's souls for the events of the trial of the Antichrist. For those, who are listening to My prompting, I am fortifying the faithful with a spiritual strength, to do battle with the demons. Even as you speak out this weekend, invoke my grace and power in your speech and guidance. It is the Lord's messengers that are being commissioned, to wake up the people from their spiritual sleep. It is time to understand the battle of good and evil that is going on in everyday life. Call on God's help in this time, since you cannot make it on your own. Shed your pride, since you will be fighting a power of evil beyond man's capability. Follow the path I give you in your work, and you will see My protection from evil is overwhelming the demons."*

Thursday, October 17, 1996: (St. Ignatius of Antioch)
After Communion, I could see Maria E. and she was welcoming some pilgrims. Then I saw a stockade and someone inside was being marched to their death as a martyr. Jesus said: *"My people, you have seen in today's readings how many of My prophets and messengers have been martyred in the past. These men and sometimes women have been a challenge to the authorities, since the authorities could not deny the truth of their words. They could not allow these messengers to continue preaching these truths, since it threatened the rulers' lives in sin and their authority before the people. Do not be surprised then, that the Antichrist will*

seek martyrdom for all of My current messengers. Satan will not have his kingdom divided, so he will silence all vocal opposition. Again, this is reason to seek hiding, but also see there is a threat to all those who speak out in My Name. My messengers must continue to seek saving souls, even if the shadow of death looms over their work."

Later, at the prayer group, I could see a king dressed in luxurious robes and then Clinton's face came to me. Jesus said: *"My people, even though your president considers himself invincible, you will see him humbled in a short time. All those, who serve the evil one, will have their day of reckoning. His reign, like the Antichrist's, will be brief until I touch him for his transgressions, especially in his dealings favoring abortion."* I could see some people erecting some grey election booths. Jesus said: *"My people, there is still time for some revelations to occur that could influence the elections. If they are not coming forward before the election, they will definitely come forward after the election. Should your current president continue with his anti-God plans, your country will suffer for his actions. If your abortions do not diminish and you do not convert yourselves, many severe chastisements will increase, such to bring you to your knees in prayer. You, My people, are controlling your destiny by your actions."* I could see a large hall of empty baby cribs. This represented those aborted who would not ever use a crib. Jesus said: *"My people, see in this vision how your abortions are frustrating my plans for these babies that will never be born. I have told you to treat life as something very precious and preserve it in all of its forms. Satan is trying to destroy all those whom he can entice in aborting their children. Listen more to your hearts than your wallets when you are making decisions about life."* I could see some tall walls of a new prison under construction but it was open to the outside from within. Jesus said: *"My people, your future captors are building a vast gulag of prisons to hold all those who refuse to go along with the new world order of the Antichrist. Some of this information has leaked out, but there are Satan's agents preparing their new torture chambers for the Christians. Do not fear, My people, but seek My help in the coming trial. You must come to Me in faith if you are to be saved. Some will be persecuted, but I will protect many at My refuges and those in hiding. My angels will fight your battles if you call on them."* I could see some food jars that people were carrying with them. Jesus said: *"My people, this time of famine will be severe, and I will provide for you during the tribulation. I have asked you for full trust in Me to provide for you with My manna from heaven. I will show My mercy on those weak in faith by perpetuating your meager food supplies of what you bring. In this way you will be fed in your desperation. Pray, My people, that you will have the strength to endure this trial I am testing you with. This is all a part of your purification, so you will be pleasing to Me when I invite you to my wedding feast."* I could see Mary and she had a covering over her nose because the stench of our sin was offending her. Mary said: *"My dear children, your sins have me crying continuously, since you are not listening to my messages. If you were listening, there would be enough prayer to combat the evils in your country. How many times will my pleas for conversion fall on deaf ears? My children, you must pray your Rosaries and work to save those souls around you. Many are not changing their lives, as they are headed straight for the abyss of hell, if they do not turn back. Wake up my children to their evil ways, and show them to my Son where they can confess their sins and be saved."* I could see some Christmas trees and other traditions of the crib scene. Jesus said: *"My people, many are refusing to believe in Me as men try to remove My Commandments, and any other remembrances of Me in public. As your pagan gods of money and earthly distractions throttle your soul, your chance for conversion is slipping away. You do not have much time to turn around your love to Me. Listen and come to Me, or the demons will be carrying you off to hell."*

Friday, October 18, 1996: (St. Luke)
After Communion, I could see someone preaching. Jesus said: *"My son, this is a fitting day that you should be preaching My Gospel. Call on My help and that of the Holy Spirit, to speak My Words with authority. This is a crucial time in preparing the people for this test of evil in My purification. As in the Gospel, preach My message of peace, love and conversion. Those with open hearts will receive your message. Pray for those who will not listen, and*

seek their conversion through My forgiveness in confession. Some may not believe in My messengers, but they must listen to the truth of My words. If the people do not repent of their sins, then Satan will gather them into his hands. You are fighting in a battle for souls. Do not leave one possibility closed, in order to bring these souls to Me. Show them the urgency of My message, as the tribulation is about to descend on all of mankind."

Later, I could see Jesus come with His arms outstretched, and He showed me some empty pews in a Church. Jesus said: *"My son, I am grateful to you for carrying out My Will in following your mission. I am especially thankful, for all of your prayer requests with the people afterwards. My message of love and hope has fallen on good ground, where it will yield much fruit. Continue in your work unceasingly, for there are many souls that need to be brought back to My church. You are seeing a fulfillment in your public ministry that will be a beacon of faith for the people. Continue in your prayers to keep yourself humble and strong, and give Me all the praise and thanks for the gifts I pour out on you. Your thank you for all of My gifts has touched My heart by your helping all of these people."*

Saturday, October 19, 1996: (St. Isaac Jogues and companions)
After Communion, I could see a road going into the distance. Jesus said: *"My son, you are seeing a path for your mission to My faithful. This is the road to evangelization I ask of all My messengers. Your accepting My Will to teach My words is a means to your salvation as well. Give glory and praise to Me for all of these gifts that I am sharing with you. As I travelled from town to town to bring My kingdom to all who would listen, so I ask you to travel as well, like the missionaries being honored this day. Those, who spread My Word to instill love and conversion in the hearts of My people, will receive a prophet's reward. Go as I taught My apostles and preach My word to all nations."*

At Nocturnal Hour, I could see a picture of all the men and women at their desks in the House of Representatives. In the next scene, they were all gone and they were replaced with black round disks. Jesus said: *"My people, you have squandered all the gifts that I have given you, and you are now more taken up with your pride and your greed. Your country was founded on righteous principles with God-centered motives. Today, this United States is overrun with too many avaricious factions, all seeking government hand outs. Men's greed for power will be his undoing. As the tribulation comes closer, you will see your country dismantled as you know it. Control of your country will be replaced by tyrants who will be faithful only to the Antichrist. Many have sold their souls to Satan in the one world government. Soon your government will be taken over by secret UN troops who have been years planning this coup. You will see circumstances change quickly, so that you will have to go into hiding for fear of your lives. Gestapo tactics will be employed to bring everyone into submission and make them ready to accept the mark of the beast. You must flee this foreign force and seek My help, so you can hide from them. Pray for My help and I will send My angels to watch over you. In the end, My power will reign supreme, so do not fear this short time of Satan's reign."*

Sunday, October 20, 1996:

After Communion, I could see some crops growing in rows, symbolizing the faithful. I then saw a snake slithering among the crops, and finally I could see a spear stab the snake. Jesus said: *"My people, you are made in My image and I have given each of you many talents, so you can flourish to yield thirty, sixty, and a hundred fold. Your destination is to bear much fruit in faith, and to be gathered up into My barn in heaven. This portrayal of My faithful is timely, since you are witnessing the time of harvesting souls is upon you. I am the Harvest Master and I am sending My priests and messengers to seek out sinners and bring them back to Me. In this evil age, you also are seeing the serpent misleading My people, by distracting them with the ways of the world instead of My ways. I seek out each soul to its dying day, and I shower my rain of love on each of you, to allow you to grow in love of Me. I give you hope even in this troubled time, that I will defeat Satan with ease, and he will then be removed from the earth. I encourage My people to persevere through your trial with My help, and I will bring you to a land of milk and honey. There your spirit will have rest and My love will consume you."*

Later, at St. George's Church in Niagara Falls, N.Y. during the rosary and exposition, I saw a small spotlight searching through the darkness. Jesus said: *"My people, many of you are searching for a peace and rest in your soul. You go about life seeking to satisfy the senses, but you never find fulfillment from anything that is earthly. You may find something that may please you for a time, but it soon passes and again you still seek satisfaction. As I told the woman at the well, the water you drink, you will need again. I will give you living water, when you drink of My Spirit. It is I, who give you Myself in Holy Communion under the appearances of bread and wine. I am the only One who will satisfy your soul, since I have the words of eternal life. Come to Me, My people, and I will give you rest and peace for your soul. I am the one your soul thirsts for, since I am the creator that your spirit must be a part of. You are one with My Mystical Body. That is why you cannot have life apart from Me. Seek Me always, and you will be one with Me in My Divine Will in Heaven."*

Monday, October 21, 1996:
After Communion, I could see a small crack with black material oozing out. Gradually, this crack became a huge hole with a cesspool of black coming out. Jesus said: *"My people, you are seeing an evil age come to its peak, as the final years of tribulation are about to complete this age. You think that evil has increased rapidly, and it has. You will see that evil will have a short reign, and grow worse even for these coming years. I tell you, take heart in My love, that I am coming to judge this evil lot. Many injustices are occurring, as the evil one is having his day. I tell you, his kingdom is not long for this earth. I will soon settle accounts, and those who have defied Me will pay for their crimes. I am a loving and merciful God, but My justice cries out to bring My wrath on these evil doers. Have faith in Me, My people, and soon you will have your reward in my abundant graces."*

Later, at adoration, I could see a reliquary holding the miracle of the Body and Blood of Jesus at Lanciano, Italy. Jesus said: *"My people, I have died for all of mankind that you may be saved by the ransom of My Death on the cross. My Real Presence will be with you even during the coming tribulation. Those, who are spiri-*

tually hungry, and those with physical hunger, should pray to Me and their angels to send My heavenly manna. Wherever My faithful will reside, either in hiding or in detention centers, I will bring My Presence to all who pray to receive Me. When you cannot receive Me physically, I ask that you pray for a spiritual communion, and I will be with you. See the gift of My Presence is necessary to sustain your strength in your spiritual life at all times. I will not leave you orphans, but see I am a prayer away from you. Have trust in me that I love all of you so much, that I will guard your souls at all times, especially during the trial. I give you this hope, so you will be able to endure what may seem impossible to overcome. My joy and peace go with you wherever My faithful are joined in prayer.

Tuesday, October 22, 1996:

After Communion, I could see a dome of light and it turned around and pointed in all directions around the earth. I then saw immediately after, a picture of tunnels and caves. Jesus said: *"My people, beware of the angel of light, who will come claiming to be Me. I have warned you in My Scriptures of the false witnesses who will come at the last days claiming to be the Christ. Do not believe them, since you will know when I come on a cloud, it will be with glory you will fully understand. The Antichrist will show a false peace, make miraculous claims, but all will be illusions. When you are visited with these happenings, it is truly time to hide from this evil power. Call on Me and I will have your angels lead you to safety. You will know this is a battle of good and evil. The Antichrist will not be a man of love, but only one desiring control over the people by his power of suggestion."*

Later, I could see many people in a line in a hall waiting to be interrogated. The next scene was at night and I could see several columns of dark silhouettes being marched down the road. It was revealed to me that these were the people marked to be eliminated. Jesus said: *"My people, I wish to give you a serious warning to all who love Me and are faithful to My Word. At the coming of the tribulation, the Antichrist's agents will be preparing the way by identifying all those who are Christians, or those who would defy his takeover. When his time comes, you will see his people gather all of these targeted for elimination very quickly. They will be sent to death camps as in previous wars to be tortured or exterminated. It is important, My people, to be on the watch at this time for the beginning of the tribulation, to know when you will be sought out. I will give you a warning when to go into hiding before these agents can capture you. Pray for My guidance and help at this time, since many lives will be taken in this first stage. This will be a dark hour in man's history, and I will be guarding your souls from these evil men and demons. Keep faith in Me, and I will bring you to My joy in the era of peace that follows. Trust in Me, that this time of evil will be short, and My victory will conquer all of this evil lot in an inkling of time. Protect your souls with prayer, since your soul is your most prized possession."*

Wednesday, October 23, 1996:

After Communion, I could see some straw and a fire burning out of control. It was revealed that this was a reference to the recent fires out West. Jesus said: *"My people, I give you earthly gifts and I take them away. Do not build up elusive wealth only for yourself, since there is never any security in your own deeds. You can see the things that you have, can be taken away at any time, as with these recent fires. Do not depend on your wealth, but place your dependence on Me. Trust in My help that I will provide for your needs both physically and spiritually. Remember, that apart from Me, you are nothing. So do not be disappointed if you are not successful in the world's eyes, for you are here to do your best for Me and not for any selfish interests. Elusive wealth is not to be sought of its own, but use your talents for My Will and you will be rich in heavenly gifts that no one can take from you."*

Thursday, October 24, 1996:

After Communion, I could see some satellites being propelled into orbit. Jesus said: *"My people, I am showing you some recent low orbiting satellites being sent up, for the purpose of surveillance and mapping. They are being placed lower, so their infrared sensors and cameras can trace people's movements. Such electronic devices will be used by the Antichrist, to find people and locate there whereabouts. Even though many such devices will be used by evil men, I can thwart them in their evil efforts to control the people. I have told you that I will confuse the proud and raise the lowly. You will see My powers in action, so that I will protect many of My faithful from the demons. This is because I will never let you get tested beyond your endurance. This is a hopeful protection that I will offer to anyone in prayer and those following My Will. You will see miraculous things happen through My angels to control the evil about you.*"

Later, at the prayer group, I could see a man carrying a cross on his back. Jesus said: "*My people, I call on all of you to take up your cross and carry it with Me. I have suffered as you must suffer in your trial on earth. You may be severely tested in life, especially in the end times. I will help lead you to safety and I will watch over you daily. The world is in need of purification and I will bring it about in My time. My love and mercy go out to all of you.*" I could see more flames around the land as it consumed the vegetation. Jesus said: "*My people, your sins are scorching the earth with evil, as the lifeblood of your faith is being tested. See in these flames how evil leaves everything lifeless behind it. You, My faithful, must bring My peace and love back into your cold world before it is fully consumed.*" I could see some farm machinery moving down some main roads. Jesus said: "*My people, your chastisements on the land may force farmers to move to new land to farm. Your current farms are suffering droughts and floods. You would be wise to find more land to farm instead of building, or you may not have enough to eat. This equipment is going down the main road, since soon growing food will be difficult and it will be desperately needed. Pray to Me that your harvests improve as your prayer increases.*" I could see rows of rich wheat fields being harvested. Jesus said: "*My people, I am showing you the harvests you are used to, but they will be less as you depend on yourselves alone. You fail to realize, that all you are given, comes from Me. I am the one who makes the seed grow and flourish. If you want rich harvests, you need to root out the seeds of evil in your society. Until you listen to Me and pray for My help, your food will be sparse and you will go wanting.*" I could see a man steering a large wheel on a ship. Jesus said: "*My people, your country has been turned into evil waters that are buffeting you with all manner of trials. You are the ones who can chart your course in life. If you continue to take a course away from Me, you will be leaving My blessings behind, and you will be on your own. Come to Me now, My people, or you will soon perish in the hands of the evil one. I keep sending you many messages to wake up your spirit and place your trust in Me. Without Me you are nothing and you will be swallowed up in your sins. With Me you will find my bounty of graces to lead you to your salvation.*" I could see a sky full of lights and wonders. Then I could see the Antichrist come forward sitting on a throne. Jesus said: "*My people, when you see the Antichrist come, do not be taken in by his signs and appearing miracles. He is the father of lies and illusions. Do not listen to him in any way. Instead, hide from him in anyway possible, for his influence will challenge even the elect. Seek My mercy and My help during this trial, for I will be your only way to be saved. You will not survive spiritually or physically on your own, but with Me, you will be protected.*" I could see Mary come and she was pushing someone in a wheelchair. Mary said: "*My dear children, thank you for your Rosaries, because it is through them, that I can help sinners who are spiritually sick. You also, can help people directly by your good deeds and your good example. Help your neighbor in his need physically, and lead them to Jesus to help them cleanse their souls. By your going to confession, you give example to others when you confess your sins. Lead lives in keeping with my Son's commands and again you will lead others to my Son by your example. Help sinners to be saved in any way you can with our help in prayer.*"

Friday, October 25, 1996:
    After Communion, I was looking down on a green football field and I understood again the connection with the coming warning. Jesus said: "*My people, this again is a reminder to you of My warning, which is not far off. Do not be disappointed if life does not continue on as you are used to it. In order for My purification of the earth to be effective, there must be some dramatic changes. You know that you are in the end times, by the many signs I send to you. Also, I go before you to prepare My people with a mercy, only I can provide. You must make room for Me in*

your heart, and seek forgiveness of your sins in confession. Repent and convert now, while there is time. Brace yourselves for My warning, which will be a startling experience to see all of your lives as I would see them in judgment. Have faith that this preparation will be received by all of mankind. Heed the meaning of this warning and change your life around to Me, before it is too late to be saved."

Later, I could see a cross and then blue lights of the world. These scenes alternated several times. Finally, I could see events speeding up as time was moving faster. Jesus said: *"My people, I bring you a message of hope even amidst the adversity around you. You, My children, are no different than My people of Israel. You have been given many gifts, but over time you have come to expect them. I give my blessings to those who love and seek Me. Lo, you think you can do many things without My help. You still do not understand My gifts and the praise and thanks that I deserve. Instead, you want to take the credit for your good fortunes, and look away from Me for thanks. For those, who think all good things come from them, you will see dismal failure when I withdraw My hand from you but a moment. See that everything you have comes from My bounty. Come to Me out of love to give Me praise for My glory. Convert your lives now, for your time grows short. As you see events speed up, know that the end times are upon you. Just as you thought you had enough worldly goods for years to come, I will come with My purification to jolt you out of your sinful ways, so you may fall on your knees and adore Me. For those, who choose the Antichrist and worldly comforts, you will lose what little you have, and understand that this world is passing away. Do not place your trust in something that is temporary, but seek Me now and I will bring you everlasting life."*

Saturday, October 26, 1996:

After Communion, I could see the tomb where Jesus was buried. Jesus said: *"My people, I am the resurrection and the life. No one comes to heaven, unless they come through Me, for I have died that all of you may have life everlasting. Since Adam's sin, all of you have been appointed to die as a consequence of original sin. Also, you were steeped in sin and death until My Resurrec-*

tion. You are still weak in your sins, but now I offer you salvation by My saving power of the cross. I have ransomed you from your sins, but you must repent and seek My forgiveness in confessing your sins. Give glory and thanks to your loving God who holds out his hand to carry you all to heaven. I love you, my people, and I do everything to lead you to me. For those who honor Me in prayer, I will protect you from evil. Seek your Lord every day, and My Father will give you your eternal reward in heaven. Love one another, and lead all souls to Me, your Creator."

Later, after Communion, I could see an underground crypt with a corridor and there were many little caskets moving along in a procession. Jesus said: *"My people, what you are seeing is a proper burial rite given for your many abortions. It is bad enough that you are killing your babies, but still your society has yet to accept that they are even human. When you declare it a human at birth, at which point in your own development do you consider yourself less than a human? You are human from conception, since you came from human parents. Your society denies the unborn is human, so it can justify taking their lives. This killing is a grievous sin, and it becomes a sin against the spirit, even more so, when you refuse to accept it as a sin of murder. If you are to be saved, these sins must be confessed and forgiven. Even many women suffer from their guilt, since deep down they sense a guilt from their loss of their unborn children. Come to Me and I will forgive even your worst sins, but come. If you fail to seek My forgiveness or rationalize it is not a sin, you will be condemned at the judgment. It is this attitude of your abortion acceptance, that calls down My wrath on your nation. All of your good deeds are overwhelmed with this carnage of your abortions, and especially for those accepting blood money for profits. If you see My chastisements fall upon you, know that your ruthless killing of babies has brought it upon you. This is the most serious sin you can commit against My laws, so see that it is so important to stem the tide of this killing or your country will cease to exist."*

Sunday, October 27, 1996:

After Communion, I could see vast numbers of people sitting in an audience. Jesus said: *"My people, you are craving for a deep-*

ening in your spirituality, but many pulpits are not speaking forth to provide a vibrant faith. Instead of dwelling too much on a social gospel agenda, it is better to teach about making everyone whole in spirit and body. You are made to My image, so it is important that you give Me praise and thanks in prayer every day, and not just on Sunday. My faithful need to be encouraged to have a good prayer life, so they may be strengthened every day to do My Will. My people are craving the sacred in My Real Presence in Holy Communion. You should give me respect in My Presence, and make regular visits to My tabernacle to give Me adoration. You need to confess your sins regularly in private confession, to keep your soul vibrant with grace and unclouded with any mortal sin. Even the mention of sin is rarely heard in homilies. Without proper formation of conscience on sin or a renewal of the truths of your faith, how can My faithful maintain their spiritual health? It is time My friends to pray for your priests, that they may be bold in their teaching, and bring My faithful closer to the one true faith given you by My apostles. It is for this reason, that My faithful are not being properly fed, that I am bringing forward many messengers to help wake up the true faith in My people. Many faithful have grown cold in their religion by not practicing what they read in the Scriptures. Come to me now and be transfused with a deeper love for Me, so you can perfect yourself in getting ready to be with Me in heaven."

Later, at Our Lady of Fatima Shrine near Lewiston, I could see several crescent objects faced toward a large flame as in pagan worship to earthly gods. Jesus said: *"My people, I alone am the one God. All other gods are not of Me and are distractions for your soul. All gods of the earth, crystals, money, material goods, sports, or any other persons are not to be adored. Anything, which you spend many hours with, will soon become a god for you. Be careful how you spend your time. Think to please Me in every way possible by taking away all of your distractions. Resolve to do everything for Me and you will avoid many occasions of sin. Remember I am the only one to pay homage to and I ask you to give me praise as your God. See I am the reason for your life to know, love and serve me. Once you see I am the only One to give your allegiance, even over your own desires, then you will want to give your will over to My Divine Will. Seek Me every day this way, and I will bring you along the path to heaven."*

Monday, October 28, 1996: (Sts. Simon & Jude)
After Communion, I could see my Aunt Annette come to speak to me on the day of her Mass intention. Aunt Annette said: *"I am happy to see all of my family on the Leary side. Thank you all for coming to my mass intention and pray for me. I have many great memories with all of you, and I was happy to be able to share my life with you. Thank you also, for all that you did for me in life."*
Later, I could see kings strutting through the streets in robes of splendor. Then, I saw these same rulers in tattered clothes. The Holy Spirit came and said: *"I am the Spirit of love and you can feel My presence here tonight, even as you saw the flames flow tall on the candles. Many prophets and messengers are tested by the authorities and some, like the apostles, were tortured and martyred. These same figures in authority have later come to a bad end because of their evil deeds. I call on all of you to live the message of Jesus and go out to all the nations and spread the Gospel message. This time is ever ripe for evangelization to bring the people back to God. For those who come forth in this calling, know that My grace will be with you in your speech. I will enable you through My gifts to bring God's love to all open hearts that will receive Us (Trinity). I will give you courage also to endure all hardships that may befall you in your service to the Lord. See My grace is pushing you forward to be an instrument of God so that all men will be blessed with the knowledge of salvation in the Gospel. Listen, all of mankind to the Word of God being brought to you through My many messengers."*

Tuesday, October 29, 1996:
After Communion,, I could see a large opening in a cave and there was a brilliant light as at the Resurrection. Jesus said: *"My people, I am showing you in this vision, a picture of the resurrection of the people. I am the light at the end of the tunnel, that all mankind seeks. When Satan is defeated, I will show you the splendor of My victory. The dead will be in their glorified bodies, as I have promised you. When evil is conquered, only my love and*

*goodness will permeate everything on their way to perfection.
See all power resides in Me over the good and the bad. At that
time all will be judged on the merits of their love for me. Woe to
those when the master comes and they are not found watchful. I
tell you, those who become lost in the world and are not ready to
come to heaven, will be judged unworthy and cast into the fires
of Gehenna. Those, who are like the five wise virgins and make
ready for my appearance, will go forward into my banquet both
on earth and in heaven."*

Later, I could see some people climbing mountains in the wilderness. Then, they were seeking to hide among the woods. Jesus said: *"My people, you are seeing how you must flee the Antichrist's agents to avoid being placed in detention centers. I am reminding you that they will search for you with satellites and helicopters, using many electrical sensing devices. You must pray to Me and your angels that we will block their finding you. Those who are faithful to Me, I will protect from all of these demonic forces. You will see My power will overshadow anything that Satan will devise. Even though you think it impossible to avoid these evil forces, I will perform miracles to protect you. Take hope, My children, I will be watching over you in spiritual and physical matters. Even amidst evil men, I will thwart their designs on you. I will only allow those intended by My Will to be martyred. The rest will be miraculously cared for. You will not have seen such open protection, since the days I helped My people in the Exodus. This purification time will be shown to be a battle of good and evil that has been destined for centuries."*

Wednesday, October 30, 1996:

After Communion, I could see an evil eye opening, as if from the Antichrist. With his gaze came a hypnotizing power that reached out into the whole world. This vision seemed to indicate the beginning of his power. Jesus said: *"My people, this vision is a warning again of this evil age coming to its peak with the public appearance of the Antichrist. This evil appearance will be one showing miracles and powers such that you should avoid his presence by hiding. When he controls TV and even radio, he will be able to induce evil by the power of his charisma and the power of suggestion. It will be impossible to survive this time without dependence on My help. Only those, strong in Me, will be able to resist this force. You will see My power unleashed through My angels that will hold him in check from attacking My faithful. Prepare now, My friends, for the onslaught of this evil power which will come soon. Return to Me and convert your lives so you will be able to defend yourselves with My armor, and the help of your guardian angels."*

Thursday, October 31, 1996:

After Communion, I could see Maria E. and she was looking down. Then, I could see some pumpkins and witches symbolizing evil powers. Jesus said: *"My people, do not give more credit to the devil's power than he deserves. I hold his power in check, since all he can do is what I allow. Remember, My power is above all powers. Every person and being must personally answer to Me only. If evil has any seeming control over events, it is more a result of the sins of men. The devil can tempt, but it is man who carries out any sinful action. If you are seeing more evil today, it is because your society allows it, more than Satan's power. Just as evil has increased, it can decrease if enough good people change their lives back to following My ways, instead of those of the world."*

Later, at the prayer group, I could see masks of people's faces on the roofs of each house. Jesus said: *"My people, this is an appropriate day that you take off the masks of your worldly airs and put on the faith you know and love. It is important that your appearance to others is one of joy in the Lord at all time. You have hope in being a resurrected people. So do not put on your sad face of complaints or worldly airs that you are more important than you are. Give good example to others by following what I have given you in the Gospels."* I could see a roundabout way to get into the Church door. Jesus said: *"My people, come to me through the narrow gate that the world refuses to follow. I ask that you live humbly and in submission to My Will. It is not easy to deny yourself and turn away from worldly delights. Still your soul yearns to be with Me, and it is this narrow road of faith in Me, that I ask each of you to follow. See that you are dependent on Me for everything, and do not think you can do anything on your own."* I could see some homeless people sleeping on park benches. Jesus said: *"My people, do not be critical of others whom you may dislike. There are some in worse states than yourselves, but do not belittle their status. I see all of you equally as a human soul in My Kingdom. Treat your neighbors as an equal and help those in need, especially with your surplus. When you help the least in My Kingdom, you are helping Me. Also, do not talk about others behind their back, so you may not ruin their names. In many such instances treat others with kindness as you expect to be treated.*" I could see some armored vehicles preparing for war on a hill. Jesus said: "*My people, many times I have asked you to pray for peace in your world. By your greed for wealth and land, many are making war plans for their own control over things. Put aside your anger and your worldly desires, and ask for My true peace. Seek Me and My ways, and you would have no need for wars. Put aside your hatreds of your neighbor for any reason. Instead, make amends with your brother before you bring your gifts to Me at the Altar.*" I could see some people set aside some food for some future emergency. Jesus said: "*My people, some have been critical of My messages to save some food for the coming famine. Those, who are critical, are storing up other worldly treasures of lesser value. When you die, to whom will this piled up wealth go to? You cannot seek luxuries in this life and criticize others for being more prudent. Life is a test for you, not just to be enjoyed in wanton pleasure. Pray that you will understand the narrow road to Me, I ask you to follow, rather than following the broad road to hell.*" I could see some people dressed in army uniforms, but they were in a vague yellow shadow. Jesus said: "*My people, I am showing you that there are secret armies around you in places you do not expect. Be aware that the Antichrist is making his plans behind the scenes, and he will take over with a suddenness you cannot imagine. Prepare for this time, so when it occurs, you will be ready to go into hiding. I remind you that this is a battle of good and evil where you will have My angels to fight for you. Do not take up arms in any killing, for this is what Satan desires.*" I could see Mary with a crown making ready for her visit to Purgatory where she lifts up those souls ready for Heaven on these feast days of All Saints and All Souls. Mary said: "*My dear children, I ask you to pray for these poor souls in Purgatory, who are many times neglected, even by their own relatives. Have mercy on their suffering, even as I go to relieve their suffering a little, by showing them love and quenching their thirst for the sight of the divine, which they see in my Son who comes with me. When you pray for sinners, include the poor souls as you double your intentions.*"

Friday, November 1, 1996: (All Saints' Day)

After Communion, I could see a white veil of light with two young people dressed in white. Then, I saw an old woman bent over coming to the young people. Jesus said: *"My people, this is a glorious day because you are seeing where you are being directed after death. All of your suffering and struggling to please me is rewarded in your coming to heaven as a saint. You have many great saints as models for your lives. Remember them in your prayers and ask them to help you, even now. Every faithful, who makes reparation for their sins, is entitled to be with Me as I have promised you. Many unknown saints are being welcomed. As long as you love Me sincerely and follow My Will, you too, can come among My saints. Sainthood is your goal and should be sought by everyone. It is very achievable, if you would give your will over to Me. You must lose your life in order to save it. Come join Us in heaven, where We await all those seeking My banquet."*

Later, I could see a group gathered for some service and they were all crowded around in a circle. I could see lights and flames with a large object in the middle. Jesus said: *"My children, what you are witnessing is a seance in worshipping the evil one. You should know that just as many prayer groups are forming, there are also many worshipping in black masses or channeling. Just as goodness in faith and My graces come forth at these times in your prayer groups, so also, more evil is coming forth from the evil forces in the black masses. With their channeling, information is being passed by the force of the dark side in Satan's camp. This again, is where the battle lines for souls are being drawn. As you understand these happenings going on, you must realize that more prayer to fight evil is now necessary to combat these covens. Do not think that since you do not see these actions, there is nothing going on. I tell you, you will need My graces more now than ever to protect your souls from this evil influence. Say your prayers of exorcism often to hold these evil forces in check."*

Saturday, November 2, 1996: (All Souls' Day)

After Communion, I could see a grey area under a picture of Heaven that was in gold. This was the dome of Purgatory's presence. I then could see a sort of pit to climb down as it was a break away portion to show the souls suffering in a dingy dark place. These souls were all crying out for help. Jesus said: *"My son, you are seeing in this vision how many are still suffering for their sins. I have made this real for you, so you can witness to everyone that truly this place, you call purgatory, does exist. It is truly a place of reparation for the temporal punishment due your sins. Those, who do not have their suffering on earth for their sins, will have to be purified in this place of torment. In the upper levels of purgatory as you see, the worst suffering is to be without My presence. There is open to you an option to suffer for your sins on earth. Some of those, who suffer much before death, have gained heaven in this way. Pray for these poor souls regularly to alleviate their suffering. Especially, remember to pray for your own relatives and friends."*

Later, at Adoration, I could see some heavy snow banks on the road. Jesus said: *"My people, I am showing you a heavy snowfall, so you can get used to this sight. You have seen several years of higher than average snowfall, and this winter season will be no different. Many forecasts have said your winter will be severe and that it will be. I have tested you much with the weather and fires as well. How long will it take for you to understand the connections between the increase in evil with the increase in winter severity? I tell you, My people, you must change your lives and convert now. No longer will you have the luxury of time. Come to Me and I will give you My rest. If you remain lazy in your sin and avoid confession, then you give the evil one a chance to weaken and steal your soul. Show Me your love by making a serious commitment to better your lives, and I will send you my grace to complete your conversion."*

Sunday, November 3, 1996: (Mass for Parish's Deceased in last year)
After Communion, I could see a living Jesus come forth and raise His arms among the people present in a blessing. Jesus said: *"My people, I come to add My blessing over the people for their intentions. You are to know that those souls in heaven and purgatory are all a part of My One Body of faithful. Those souls, who are condemned to hell, are no longer accepted members, since they have rejected My call. As you make a remembrance of these souls,*

never forget them and pray for them continually through the years. Many are suffering in purgatory longer, since their relatives have forgotten them. Pray also for those souls who have no one to pray for them. I want to remind all of you to be ever watchful over your own souls, so you may be ready for your own death. Some have called this time a tribulation, that leads up to the time of the Antichrist. I tell you, when the evil one has his brief reign, you will truly know the meaning of the word tribulation. What you are experiencing now, is nothing compared to those days of the real tribulation. Prepare, My souls, but have faith and hope that I will protect you. My resurrection is a sign to you, that all of My faithful will be resurrected in the glory of heaven where you will love and praise Me forever."

Later, I could see four traces of gold light streak across the skies. It was revealed that these were four angels of the end times. Jesus said: *"My people, the angels, you are seeing, are a sign that the end times are almost upon you. These are the angels who will bring the famine, pestilence and plagues. It is time for them to come to the earth with each of their missions to chastise the earth. Many have not wanted to believe these things will happen. Prepare your souls now, My friends, for soon your testing will become severe. Those, without belief in Me, will be shaken by these events. They will be forced to believe in the end times as it happens before them. Satan will claim all those souls who refuse Me and accept the mark of the beast. He will control and torture all those who go with him, for he hates all men. Be forewarned that unless you seek Me for help, you will never see eternal life in heaven. Trust in Me, and My protection will envelop your soul. Your life leads you to Me in many ways. It is up to you to accept Me and bring Me into your heart, if you are to be saved."*

Monday, November 4, 1996:

After Communion, I could see some green rock. I then saw a cave hollowed out in a perfectly cut oval shape. Jesus said: *"My people, I am showing you the grace of My protection in carving out caves for you. You may be offended that I am leading you to such places, yet they are the best place for your protection. Some still do not believe this is necessary, but when the tribulation be-*

gins, you will be thankful I have looked out for your welfare. Believe Me, My friends, the evil men will cause My faithful much difficulty. You will see persecution at such a pitch, that these men will seem like demons to you. Pray much for My help during this trial and you will not be disappointed in My watching over you. It is only through My help, that you will be brought through this terror of evil. Do not underestimate Satan's desire to try and control all of mankind, but have hope since My power far surpasses any of his designs."

Later, after Communion, (Bob Schaeffer's Funeral), I could see a picture frame and it was completely black inside. In the next scene I could see many pink roses all inside the picture frame. Finally, I could see a beautiful bridge with yellow leaves of fall all around and a bright shining sun. Jesus said: *"My people, in this black picture you are seeing death as a consequence of sin. You can place all of your pictures here, since you are all appointed to die one day. As you see roses come, this is a sign that I will raise all of you up in My resurrection of the faithful. You will then become one with the communion of saints. Give thanks and praise for My glorious gift of life after death. Then, you will put on your washed robes and join Me in heaven to share forever in My love and peace. You will see by this bridge, that now you will be transformed like a butterfly, from your mortal bodies to a glorified body that I intended for all men to have. Rejoice, My people, in the joy and hope of when you will be with Me in heaven. Let this close of the fall season show you life's cycle of life that will end here, but begin anew in my loving presence."*

Tuesday, November 5, 1996:

After Communion, I could see a man in a pointed hood as a monk. Jesus said: *"My people, as you see this vision of a man praying, may you consider saying your prayers in contemplative silence. Some are blessed who are in priestly orders or orders of nuns in the cloister. They pray constantly for the sins of the world in their private chapels and rooms. You, too, can take the time in your upper rooms to talk to Me in private prayer. It is often difficult to be in proper contemplation of Me when you are in the middle of your busy and rushed society. It is much better to quiet*

yourself down in private prayer, so you can meditate on the meaning of your prayers. Pray also in the quiet places of My adoration before My blessed sacrament. By taking time out of your busy day for Me, I will recognize your efforts to get close to Me, and I will send you My graces for your daily help. Those who recognize Me before men, I will recognize before My Heavenly Father."

Later, I could see a long white tomb and it had Easter colors of pink and purple decorating it. Jesus said: *"My people, this fall season is very much a reminder of the end of your life on earth. As you think of what is in the next life, focus on Me as your goal for eternity. This vision reminds you of My Resurrection, and that you are all Easter people. Think of resurrecting with Me throughout the whole year and not just on Easter. I call all of you to conversion by confessing your sins and seeking My forgiveness. I have given My life over to the Father, so all of mankind may be ransomed from their sins. The gates of heaven, which were closed to man because of original sin, are now open. It is you, by your actions and desires, that will choose between Me and the world. Temptations for sin are very strong now, as evil is prevalent in many circles. Seek My strength in grace all the more, since you will have to depend on Me during the tribulation. Come to Me now, so I can give you My peace and show you the way to be saved. You must kneel and give Me thanks and praise, so that you can give your God the proper respect that your Creator deserves. Prepare yourselves with clean souls, My friends, and I will be waiting at heaven's gate to receive you."*

Wednesday, November 6, 1996:
After Communion, I could see a closed up Church. I then saw a blue light coming over everything. I saw Jesus coming on a cloud in His glory and light shone out from Him over everything. Jesus said: *"My son, just as you are in hunger for food on your fast day, you will see a time come shortly, when it will be hard to find a Mass. There will be a spiritual hunger for My Heavenly Bread in the Eucharist. This will be a much more serious hunger than mere food. In that time of persecution I have called on you to pray for a spiritual Communion when my angel will bring you My Heavenly Manna for your spiritual food. By praying to Me, I will refresh your soul and your spiritual hunger will be satisfied in me. When I come again, you will see a great change take place over all the earth. Satan will be defeated and I will renew the earth to its former glory before the fall of Adam. Rejoice, for My day is coming soon to scatter the darkness, when all evil will be done away with. Your happiness at that time will know no bounds*

and you will give Me praise and thanksgiving for My victory. Have hope, My children, and stand straight in your trial against the evil men and demons with My help."

Thursday, November 7, 1996:

After Communion, I could see some tigers and other animals and there was a golden light on all of them. I then could see a bright burst of light coming from God. Jesus said: *"My people, you are seeing again how My loving hand will touch the animal kingdom with My coming return. The wild animals will become tame and neither will require food from lower levels. Man will also be in harmony with the animals. This vision is to show the extent of the beauty of the renewal, I will bring both for man and nature. I have shown you the enrichment of your knowledge of the plants and vegetation in the era of peace. Now, you are seeing that same touch on the animals as well. Much like I preserved the animals in Noah's time, you will see again how I will protect the animals, even through the fire of the tribulation. This again is to give you hope in seeing the results of My purification of the earth in all respects."*

Later, at the prayer group, I could see an election table and it was covered with a black velvet cloth indicating evil. Jesus said: *"My people, you have made your choice in your elections and the same people causing your problems have been re-elected. Many have speculated how to change your country's directions, but no matter who is elected, the same agenda is carried out. The one world government is controlling your leaders and they are receiving their instructions from these evil men. Pray My people for My purification to come quickly. Your country is headed for a major chastisement because you still do not treat life precious. Until your country wakes up, it may be too late to correct itself."* I could see many refugees in a war torn area in Africa as in Zaire. Jesus said: *"My people, after World War II you claimed that you would never again permit a holocaust or genocide against a given people. Now, you are seeing such carnage between various groups in Africa where many are killed or are starving to death. Life's value again is being questioned, but few are willing to take corrective action. This is the same apathy that you are seeing with your daily abor-*

tions. Until you understand Satan's attack against humanity, you will not be shocked out of your complacency. Struggle for life in your prayers and actions to justify your witness to my gift of life." I could see some spotlights in the sky and then Mother Cabrini came dressed in black. Mother Cabrini said: *"My son, do not be taken in by pride while you are going many places for Jesus. You must remain humble and close to Jesus in prayer. Continue to follow His word closely and do not let men's praise mislead you. Continue to give the praise and glory to Jesus for all the good works He may do through you. I will soon see you at My springs and I welcome you at all times. Seek My intercession and prayers to help you in your mission."* I could see a dark cloud on the horizon that was coming from some huge fires. Jesus said: *"My people, why are you so blind when you see these chastising fires out west? Again, many of the people, who bring you your movies and TV programs, are having their homes burned a second time. They did not even see my hand the first time, nor now. I have told you before how many chastisements occur where there is more sin. I am not sending destruction solely as a punishment, but to wake you up and bring you to your knees. It is in turmoil that you look at your life more closely, not when affluence has dulled your love for me. Come to me, my people, and see all that is valuable can be found in me."* I could see Mary come and she had a sad facial expression. Mary said: *"My dear children, I am indeed sad because only a few of my remnant prayer warriors are listening to my messages. I have given many messages to have all of mankind come to my Son in prayer and confession of their sins. All are being called, but few are listening. I am relying on you, my faithful little ones, to go out to your friends and neighbors and spread this message of repentance. My Son's hand is about to strike the earth to end this abomination of evil, and still many do not see the need to prepare themselves for this trial. Pray much, my children, for you will have to do double duty for those others who are not praying for peace and conversion."* I could see someone carrying a cart with his possessions across a stream, but then the waters grew higher and drowned the man. A final scene was a flash of a cave. Jesus said: *"My people, many of you think you can take all of your prized possessions wherever you please. You must lose your attachment to the things of this world or your soul will be swept into hell with the demons. Do not worry about the comforts of this life, but follow Me wherever I may lead you. Be concerned more with pleasing Me instead of piling up wealth on the earth. Your safety or your reliance on money will not help you, and instead it will drag you down. Put your trust only in Me, and I will send you all of what you will need in this life.*" I could see a beautiful land where many people were standing in awe as Jesus could be seen talking to His people. Jesus said: "*My people, you are witnessing My glory as you will see it in the coming era of peace. You will all see Me at times giving you many lessons in love. You will experience My peace and My Presence at all times. If you could but sense just a few moments of My glory, you would desire My purification to come quickly. In fact the world must be purified, for men have strayed too far from Me, much as in the days before the flood and the days of Sodom and Gomorrah. My justice and grace must come to save My elect from these evil influences. Pray much in this time and I will protect you. Trust in Me and I will lead you home to heaven.*"

Friday, November 8, 1996:

After Communion, I could see a light shining from underneath a frozen puddle of water. Jesus said: "*My people, there are many among you who are represented in this vision. These souls truly are icy cold and lacking in love for Me. In some instances those, who do not love Me, have difficulty in loving anyone. Without Me, such souls will remain as frozen hulks. It is you, My faithful remnant, who are warm and vibrant with life in Me, that must try to warm these poor souls lost in the world. It will not take long for these cold souls to see that the world will not help them find peace or rest. Worldly things will never give you any lasting love or joy. Therefore, I call out to all souls who are down and in despair, to wake up and come to your Lord. I truly have the words of everlasting life, and it is only through Me that your icy hearts will be melted with My love. Accept Me into your hearts, and My love and peace will give you rest in your soul.*"

Later, I could see many lights and rows of people playing gambling machines. Jesus said: "*My people, do not be attracted by these worldly delights. Many souls are taken up with getting rich quick schemes or seeking fame and popularity among men. Do not seek after such things, since they only satisfy you but a moment. Once you achieve a certain amount of money, you only seek to gain more. When you see wealth, it is very cold by itself and very elusive. Those, who have money, now have to keep people from stealing it from them. Do not worship money by your desire to gain it, for there is only a false sense of security in it. Instead, seek Me and My heavenly riches which money cannot buy. All that is worldly, passes away quickly, but all that is from heaven, will be everlasting. That is why you should treasure Me more than money, since I offer you a security in My love in heaven that no mortal or anything earthly can offer. Your soul seeks its Creator and to be with Me only. So do not make gods out of money or place anything else before Me. I alone am your God, who deserves your praise and thanks. Seek Me first and all else will be given you besides. Return your love to the One who loves you infinitely and unconditionally. Your reward will be to live with Me forever."*

Saturday, November 9, 1996:

After Communion, I could see a crystal as it grew outward from the center. In another vision I could see ripples go out in all directions in the water. Jesus said: *"My people, as you speak out in My Name, My words go out and touch the hearts of the people with My love. My words also speak out with authority because I am the source of all life. See, My children, wherever My Word is preached, that it is contagious and spreads out from you to many others. I am calling on My messengers at this time to spread My Gospel message of conversion and prepare the souls for My second coming. Some have heard this message before, but they have not taken it to heart, and they are still lax in their spiritual health. It is important at this time that all souls get to confession and repent, for behold the kingdom of God is at hand. Go, preach this message of repentance to all who will listen and be saved. Pry them away from their worldly pursuits and seek Me first and only as your savior."*

Later, at Leticia Villar's house (the Apostolate of the Holy Family), in Bedminster, N.J., after Communion, I could see Our Lady come holding the baby Jesus and they both were wearing crowns of gold. The room was dark but light shone out from both of them.

Mary said: *"My dear children, my motherly love goes out to all of you, and I thank you for offering up all of your rosaries to us. I bring Jesus to you in this vision as much as I lead you to Him in all I do. My dear children, I affirm that prayer is lacking in your world and if it were more abundant, you would not have all of these evil things going on. I have asked prayers from you ceaselessly, and for you to offer them up for my intentions. Hold your blessed sacramentals of your Rosary, your Crosses, and your Scapulars close to your heart. These are your most powerful weapons to fight the evil ones at all times. I bring you to my Son, and I encourage you to frequently partake of His Sacraments in confessing your sins and receiving his Real Presence in the Eucharist of His Body and Blood. I wish to say and confirm for you that this is 'Holy Ground' and many of my blessed children have visited here. Your hostess is blessed to have this gift of our presence in her house. Thank you all for coming to celebrate and pray with me and my Son. Our graces are poured out over all of you, since many are like pilgrims who come to this place. Go now and have my Son's peace rest in all of the souls and hearts of those who are open to receive us."*

Sunday, November 10, 1996:

At the Blessed Sacrament Chapel near Bedminster, N.J., before the Blessed Sacrament I could see an ornate chair in white marble with gold parts around it. Jesus said: *"My son I want you to go forth to the people and preach this message of My love and My preparation for the end times. I am sending forth many messengers to bring My faithful close to Me, and to seek as many as possible for conversion that will come forward. My grace is upon you today to speak with the power of the Holy Spirit. Tell them, it is love of Me and your neighbor that is most important. Even though I give you many warnings, do not be fearful, for fear of earthly things is from the evil one. Have confidence in My protection, that I will watch over anyone who comes to Me. I have died for all of you, that your sins may be forgiven. If you wish to benefit from My gift of this ransom, you all must come forward in prayer and frequent confession of your sins. Accept the fact that you are a sinner, and you can only be perfected through this conversion process. Give your will over to Me, if you are to seek perfection. I tell you, you are here on earth as a preparation to be in heaven one day. So you must shed your desires for the things of this life and desire only heavenly things. Now you will learn that giving Me praise and thanks constantly is the life of all who are in heaven. You must train your body to be in conformance with a joyful soul which is focused on Me only. Seek to live in the Divine Will which means doing everything for Me at every moment of the day. Come to Me with this love in your heart, and I will remold you into an acceptable, beautiful soul to be presented to My Father in heaven. Continue now in your daily devotions and keep close to Me in front of My Blessed Sacrament and in Holy Communion. I am the power in your life and all of your gifts come from Me."*

Later, at Leticia Villar's house (the Apostolate of the Holy Family), in Bedminster, N.J., after Communion, I could see a big muddy hole of dirt and water. Jesus said: *"My dear children, you worry much about your outward appearance before men. You take care not to soil your clothes, and sometimes you even try to impress others by your dress. I tell you, i look into the heart and soul for how you appear before Me. You may look beautiful outside, but inside you may be black with mortal sin. So concentrate therefore, on how you look in your soul. I call you to confess your sins to the priest, so your souls may be gleaming white. By washing your robes of sin, you will share My love and glory, and all will be able to see your love in your eyes to the soul. Be thankful for the gifts of My sacraments and my eternal forgiveness. Pray, My people, that those, who have not come to Me, may find My love in you as an example, and desire to have that glow within My faithful. Encourage your brothers and sisters, who are lost, to seek the one eternal God, so they may be saved and avoid the punishments of hell. You are made for My glory and not for your own pleasure. Come, give your will to Me, and I will give you everlasting life."*

Monday, November 11, 1996:

After Communion, I could see tongues of fire come from the Holy Spirit over a priest saying Mass. The Holy Spirit said: *"I am the Spirit of Love, and I come down on all priests to help them in how to say Holy Mass, and help them in their speech at the hom-*

ily. I give them the grace and understanding to properly explain the readings for the faithful. These tongues are the many gifts I give to each of My priests to help them in their ministry. I, especially, concur in bringing the Spirit of Jesus into the bread and wine during the transubstantiation. We as the Trinity are One, and We share Our love with all of humanity, and that love becomes more intimate in Holy Communion. Give thanks and glory to God for the blessing of His priests and Our Real Presence in the Eucharist."

Later, I could see Our Lady come and there was a blue light shining out from her. Mary said: *"My dear children, I wish to thank you for accepting to talk on my feast day. I, also want to remind you to pick up my consecration book, so you can prepare for my feast and your talk. It is good that you are doing my Son's Will to accept opportunities to spread His messages. Pray much before each talk and try to have someone praying for you, so there will be less attacks against you then. See that many of these happenings have been planned for you as my Son said he would arrange things for you. Keep humble in prayer and you will witness your sincerity. Always take any opportunity to visit my Son, and show Him how much you love Him by your words of love, and your good actions even in adversity. Pray your Rosary often, but early, so you are not sleeping in your prayers."*

Tuesday, November 12, 1996:

After Communion, I was looking up from the ground with people all around looking down at a burial. Jesus said: *"My people, one thing is appointed all of you, that you must die one day. Think of all of the funerals that you have attended, since one day it will be your turn to stand judgment. You may be concerned what people will say about you, but you will see they very quickly forget you. Now, My friends, it is more important what I think of your life than what men do. After all, I will be the judge of where you will go. When you die, it will be no surprise to anyone where they will be judged to go. The wicked and even those who do not know Me will be accursed forever in the flames of hell. If you wish to be with Me in heaven, you must develop a love for Me, that I will recognize you. This means, if you truly love Me, you will give Me praise and attention everyday as your beloved. Once, you come to Me and seek forgiveness of your sins, I will be as the father of the prodigal son and welcome you into My arms of infinite love. See that I will provide you all that you need, and apart from Me, you can do nothing. Give thanks to Me, and you will see many gifts poured out over you. It is even more important that you seek spiritual gifts of strength, more than earthly things which fade away."*

Later, I could see some headlights in a bad storm. Jesus said: *"My son, I am calling on My messengers to be the light of faith that may guide My faithful through the storms of your evil age. Many heresies and disrespect for My Real Presence are being placed before My people. If some do not pray often and seek My help, it may be difficult to discern people who are misleading My faithful. Keep on the straight and narrow path to Me in all you do, and I will reward your efforts. See, My son, that it is necessary at this time to show the people how to prepare for the attacks of this evil age. Get ready now by asking your angels how they can help you. The more you pray for help from your angels, the closer you will be to them, so they can lead you at the time of the Antichrist. I have given everyone adequate time to prepare, so take advantage of this warning to plan how you will seek My help in fighting the demons. By practicing going without food, you can learn to trust in Me as I lead you to safety. Your spiritual training now will help you in the final days of battle with the demons."*

Wednesday, November 13, 1996: (St. Francis Cabrini)

After Communion, I could see Mother Cabrini come in a black dress. Mother Cabrini said: *"My dear son, I will be most grateful to welcome you back to my shrine. This ground is a refuge for all those who are weary of life's troubles. As I welcome all travelers, I would ask you to help those less fortunate around you. Helping the poor in any way you can was my life's ambition. Encourage people not to belittle those on welfare, but to understand their trials and have mercy on them in giving them help. As food is a daily struggle for most of these downtrodden, help the many foodshelves around you. In addition to your financial aid, pray for the poor, so they will be able to endure their testing."*

Thursday, November 14, 1996:

After Communion, I could see a smoking gun on a tank. Jesus said: *"My people, look around your world and see how many factions are at odds with each other. You can see the hate in their hearts toward one another. It is then easy to understand that the least excuse can set off riots and even wars. I am asking for all men to be at peace with themselves and others. Look down as I would into these cold hearts, and send a stream of prayer into these people to warm their hearts. Until you are willing to release grudges and hatred between neighbors, you will never see peace. Pray for your leaders as well not to lead wars against each other. You must pray sincerely that My peace may come and reign in the hearts of men. If not enough prayer is forthcoming, Satan will fan the flames of war."*

Later, at the prayer group, I could see a classroom with adults as students in the chairs. A stage was in front, but it was empty. Jesus said: *"My people, I alone am your teacher, and I am asking you to follow Me as I asked My disciples. You are seeing an empty stage to indicate that I am the teacher of everyone in the world. I teach you through what I have revealed to you in the Scriptures and your traditions which have been handed down. This is why I encourage you to make a point of reading a few pages from your Bibles each day. As you go over My Words, you will keep fresh in your mind how much I love you, and how I desire all of you to come to me in adoration and praise."* I could see some people preparing food for Thanksgiving Day. Jesus said: *"My people, as you make ready for your get togethers for Thanksgiving, think of those less fortunate and give some donations to your neighbors or your local foodshelves. Give thanks to Me, also, for all you have been given both spiritually and physically. As you join your families together, make a point to smooth over any bad feelings or grudges among any family members. Make amends with your brother before you give thanks to Me."* I could see some cooks who were baking things and storing them on the shelves. Jesus said: *"My people, much as you would prepare for a meal by stocking up your shelves, I am reminding you again to gradually set aside some extra food in storage for the coming famine. Those who have tried to stock certain foods have al-*

ready seen shortages. As time goes on, those who doubt My words will be found wanting. In your want I will still be there for those who pray for My help. Be patient, and I will answer all of your prayers and needs in what I find best for you." I could see a bridge across a road. Then I saw a helicopter flying on a misty day. Jesus said: "*My people, be watchful when you see strange unmarked helicopters hovering low to investigate people. These are agents of the Antichrist and they are making preparations for his takeover in a short time. Some will carry troops, while others will be firing as in a war zone. Take care to hide from them and seek protection from them through Me and your angels.*" I could see some ribbons and wrapping paper for Christmas presents. Jesus said: "*My people, this coming Advent I am pleading for your prayers of preparation more than your concern over presents. Many fall prey to all the commercialism around my feast days. Look to the scriptures to study the real meaning that should be taking your time around these holy days. There is also a mirror image of My first coming that can direct your preparation of My second coming as well. Your readings at this time draw your attention to the end times. This is even more meaningful to you as you see these signs coming upon you even now.*" I could see a green light coming from a TV. Jesus said: "*My people, I am making you aware that in the future you will see the Antichrist control people by his power of suggestion, even through your TV. The Antichrist will use many such electrical devices, so he can control many men throughout the earth at the same time. It would be well for you therefore, as these end days come, to rid yourself of all electrical communications in your households. These will all be abused and used to control you. Keep more watch on your holy statues and icons than any things of the evil one. It is what you adorn your house with that shows where your true heart is.*" I could see Mary come and she was holding a rosary very close in front of me. Mary said: "*My dear children, I am holding my Rosary in front of you, so that you never forget to keep praying my Rosary. This is your weapon against the evil one, that heaven has presented to you. I ask you often to pray, but many make excuses and put it off until your time is gone. Think to pray for peace and conversion first, before worrying about your own agendas. If you pray first, you will be pleasing my Son and Me more for all that you do after prayer."*

Friday, November 15, 1996:

At St. Thomas More Adoration in Denver, Colorado I could see a bright white object in the sky. Then under it, I saw a large black silhouette of the Antichrist across the sky. Jesus said: *"My people, you are seeing a sign in the heavens of the coming time of the Antichrist. His time of reign is not far off. For those who do not believe in these end times, you will experience them shortly and they will test your faith. Now, it will be the coming of My purification, so that once and for all, this evil will be cleansed from your world. I love you very much, My people, and I will bring you My protection from all of this evil lot. The evil people may seem in control for awhile, but I am only allowing this as a test for you. Now, you will see the true battle of good and evil come about as each side musters its forces together. Pray much that you will be strong to resist the Antichrist."*

Saturday, November 16, 1996:

At Good Shepherd Church in Denver, Colorado after Communion I could see a dark Church inside and there was a brilliant light from near the ceiling and it shone down in the shape of a triangle of solid light. This represented the Trinity and the presence of God in His Church. I could feel physically a power of the Lord come through me as a preparation for tonight. Jesus said: *"My children, I am showing you My true power and Presence in My Church through the power of My most Blessed Sacrament. As you receive Me in Holy Communion I bestow upon you My Heavenly Bread to feed your soul with your spiritual sustenance. Look to Me, My children, for My grace and help each day you come to receive Me. Those who understand the power of the Eucharist are those who come daily to partake of My Mass. I give you this gift of Myself to all who wish to stay close to Me. Some seek worldly things, but those seeking heavenly things will find Me in the Mass every time you come. This is your most prized treasure to experience. Receive Me into your hearts and let Me lead you in everything you do each day. Now, I bring the Holy*

Spirit upon you to strengthen you and protect you from evil when you proclaim My words to the people. Pray much before and during each of your presentations, so I may work a miracle of healing in all of the hearts listening to your words. I am grateful for your carrying out the mission I have given you. You will see the reward of your labors in those hearts that come to Me by the power of the Holy Spirit. Give all the praise and glory to Me in this work and keep yourself humble in My service."

Later, at St. Thomas More Adoration in Denver, Colorado I could see several streets clogged with much snow. Then I saw many tall crucifixes in a row next to a parking lot. Jesus said: *"My people, every time that you are tested, you shy away from any suffering. If you have to endure the cold for a while, you feel it is asking too much to put up with. Testing in pain is still what shows your endurance, since man looks for an easy way out. It is difficult to know whether you will give up much for love of Me. Pray that you will be able to handle your trials and not complain that they are unfair. The more you suffer for Me, the more I will reward your efforts. You will be tested in many ways, especially through the tribulation. Learn to strengthen your resolve now over little matters, so you will have the strength to persevere during more difficult matters. If you cannot stand the persecution in the green, how will you deal with it in the dry?"*

Sunday, November 17, 1996:

At Mother Cabrini's Chapel in Colorado after Communion, I could see Mother Cabrini come in black and I marveled how young she was. I then was shown an incense light at the alcove over the spring. Mother Cabrini said: *"My son, I am grateful that you have had the opportunity to visit my springs again this year. Many times you do not know how the Lord will bring things about. Give thanks to Him for touching those hearts who were instrumental in bringing you here. Your mission of evangelization has led you to many places for Jesus to touch the hearts of His faithful in a special way. Continue in your prayers here and wherever you go, so that the Lord's graces will continue to shine on your work. The Lord is beautiful and bringing souls closer to Him is a noble task which you have generously accepted."*

Later, at Adoration, I could see a convoy of covered army trucks. In the next vision, I could see many strands of barbed wire at a detention center. Jesus said: *"My dear son, many events will be happening in your life. In all of these tests remain true to your mission no matter what the costs. It is a message I continue to repeat, that you stay close to Me in prayer and remain humble. If you receive any notice, remember to give Me all the glory, and never let your pride or other temptations sway your allegiance away from Me. You are seeing these vehicles, which will be carrying those captured. Those who refuse to take the mark of the beast or are not giving allegiance to the Antichrist will be among the captured. These trucks are taking their prisoners to the detention centers which are being readied even now. I am showing you these things, not to despair in fright, but to be forewarned to leave your homes for hiding as these signs I have given come about. Have full trust in Me that I will lead you to the refuges and save havens I have prepared for you. Do not be afraid to proclaim these messages of warning, but pray for the strength to continue speaking, even if it may endanger your life. I will bring you my Holy Spirit to defend you against the attacks of the evil ones. Your persecution will progress, but your steadfastness to making these messages public must continue even to the end. It is My Will that you seek these conversions and help wake up My faithful before it is too late."*

Monday, November 18, 1996: (Sts. Peter & Paul Dedication)
    At St. Thomas More in Denver, Colorado, after Communion, I could see a family and then a picture of a bishop leading his people. Jesus said: *"My dear people, I send you My shepherds to watch over My many families. Today, in your society the family is coming under many attacks. This is the proper unit of My Body in the Church. I have given you a model in My Holy Family, so that you have models to follow in your daily lives. An important part of your families is that you pray together, to preserve that bond of unity which is threatened by divorce. I ask you, also, to pray to preserve the holiness of My creations of new life that come forth from this holy bond of marriage. Treasure the preciousness and the sacredness of life by doing everything to avoid abortions, and*

teach others how wrong such taking of life is. Do not let the cares of this life keep your family apart, but treasure the time that you are all gifted to each other in this family setting. I love all of you, and this is an extension of My love which binds each family member to Me and each other."

Later, at Adoration, I could see a man coming out of a building dressed as someone from about thirty years ago. A strong light appeared on his head and gradually he faded away. Jesus said: *"My people, what is meant by this vision is that man's morality has changed dramatically over the years without many realizing this change. I call your attention to the permissiveness of your society in respect to chastity. Many of your movies have turned to show instant gratification in everything you do. The sins of the flesh have become rampant with many having no sense of shame in breaking My Commandments. Do you think I will allow this evil to continue? I tell you, you will see My swift justice. Go before the people as Jonah did and warn them that a great purification is about to strike the world. Tell the people to repent and make ready for My Second Coming. As much as I questioned, 'will there be any faith on the earth when I come?', show the people that if they do not repent of their sins, they will reap the punishments meant for the demons in hell. You cannot deny My justice, nor that each of you must one day make an accounting for all of your actions. If you knew the enemy was coming, you would ready your defenses. I tell you, to put on your spiritual armor, for you are about to face a battle with an evil you have yet to see. Take hope though, that My help will go before you to guard your soul."*

Tuesday, November 19, 1996:

At Adoration, I could see a large explosion in a cylindrical device. I then saw a number of men in a circle in black silhouettes. It was revealed that this represented a contrived stock market crash. Jesus said: *"My people, your greed to make big money in the stock market will soon be brought low. Many have invested in the stock market, since interest rates were held artificially low. The one world government people again will play their game to control the world's money, by taking it away in another crash, as those they created before. Do not be taken up with this greed for money,*

My friends, since all will be taken away from you either sooner or later. These evil men wish to control men by controlling the money, which they will manipulate to their advantage. In the end though, their power and wealth will be taken from them as I strike all of these evil men with My justice. Their reign will be brief as I come again to renew the earth and purify it of all evil. This event in the stock market is coming soon, so give yourself less exposure to banks and stocks, where many will go bankrupt. Trust in Me, My people, more than money or your devices. I am the provider of graces in everything you have, but I can withdraw My help at any time. Be faithful to Me through My love, and I will protect you at all times."

Wednesday, November 20, 1996:
After Communion, I could see a tunnel going down into the earth. As I seemed to be falling down, I could see serpents all around in the tunnel. Jesus said: *"My people, many souls are falling deeper and deeper into Satan's web of sin. Some do not even struggle to free themselves of life's entanglements. Beware, My friends, of letting this world's desires and pleasures lead you away from Me. I am waiting for all of My children to return to Me and seek forgiveness of their sins. You are all sinners, but unless you seek freedom from your bonds of sin, you will find it harder and harder to come back to Me. The colder your hearts become, the further you drift away from the warmth of My Divine Love. Return frequently to confession, where I will gladly receive you back into my good graces. I wish to send My blessings to all, who will give an ear to My saving words. Show your love for Me in your daily prayers, so you may fight off any temptations."*

Thursday, November 21, 1996:
After Communion, I could see a bright blue light and it seemed to descend upon the earth. After, I saw many snow storms as the weather got colder. It was revealed that this was a sign of the Antichrist's coming, and the coldness came as an indication of an evil presence. Jesus said: *"My people, My mother and many of My messengers are telling you to make ready for this time of the Antichrist. This will be the peak of Satan's reign in this man*

called the Antichrist. This blue light in the sky is another sign for his coming on earth in his public life. When you see the increased cold, this represents many souls' hearts will turn cold to Me as well. A call is going out for more prayer at this time to help defend My elect from this trauma of evil. Your consolation is that I will not allow his reign to last long. Time will speed up and I will conquer all evil with one stroke of My hand."

Later, at the prayer group, I could see Mary as a young girl and there were white flowers around her head and her dress was blue. Mary said: "*My dear children, you celebrate my presentation today and in doing so, think of how your parents brought you for baptism when you were young. This was your first encounter with my Son, as his dying on the cross delivered you from original sin. You still have the consequences of that sin, but you are given a new opportunity to gain heaven through my Son's help. Bring your children to baptism and guard over their souls as part of your responsibility of bringing them up in the faith.*" I could see a train track going off into the distance. Jesus said: "*My people, your parents have brought you to Me in baptism. They have started you out on your path to follow Me. Consider the wisdom of the faith of your parents and remain on this narrow road that you may not wander away from Me. The world entices you to take other roads to fame and fortune. I offer you eternal life which is more than the world can even try to persuade you different. Follow the yearning of your soul to Me and shut out all of the desires of the body for an easy life.*" I could see some long pillars lying prostrate on the ground. It was revealed that this represented the fall of your constitutional government. Jesus said: "*My people, for many years you have fought for your freedoms from forces in other nations. You have known stability because your government recognized Me and it had a proper moral order. Now, your morals are corrupt and you no longer treasure My Commandments. You make laws of your own liking, and cause others to follow immoral protections of all life styles. I tell you, your government will crumble under the weight of your own sins and abuses. You will see Satan's forces take over your land, and force evil ways on you for a short time. Then, My saving triumph will come, and you will witness a true peace and a freedom I will grant you."* I could see some young children in want and many were roaming about homeless. Jesus said: *"My people, you can see many displaced people in Africa without any homes. Even here, you have homeless people looking for places to stay. As you come upon this Thanksgiving weekend, make an effort to help those less fortunate than you. Those you may help today, may help you some time in the future when your good fortunes may turn bad."* I could see some old people sitting and being cared for. Jesus said: *"My dear children, you must be kind and patient in helping your older relatives. Do not forget them, but tend to their needs, since they look to you for help. Your parents have struggled for you when you were younger. Now, it is your turn to return their help. No matter how difficult it may be to take care of them, do all your care giving as a prayer to Me, so what I see in secret, I will reward you in heaven. Sharing your time and help with others is your best way to help these weak parts of the Body of my Church. Remember what you do for them, you do for Me."* I could see some dead carcasses of animals and a few human bodies. Jesus said: *"My people, prepare your bodies and your souls for the coming pestilence and famine. Your souls are more parched now than your bodies may be, since many are far away from Me. You must struggle in prayer to keep your soul healthy. This is your first duty. The body will be provided for through petition of help to Me, but those, who do not seek My help, will find starvation in the soul and the body."* I could see a mat stretcher empty that was used to carry the lame. Jesus said: *"My people, I ask you to seek the master healer in Me. I send many out in My Name as instruments of healing in the faith. Those, who pray over people, need to heal the soul first, before the body. I came to heal the sick and sinners. See how many times your ills are brought on by your own failings. When you come in faith to restore your faith in seeking forgiveness, your inner healing will precede any bodily healing."*

Friday, November 22, 1996:

After Communion, I could see a white dove flying down. Then, I could see someone talking in front of a crowd and there was a white light all around a man's head. The Holy Spirit said: *"I am the Spirit of Love and I light the way of faith. You are seeing how I come down and enlighten those who speak out the Gospel message. I am coming again as you request My help in bringing the Lord's message of love and understanding. Go forth and teach what the Lord has given you as a mission. These messages are your responsibility to make them public and heard from the rooftops. Do not hold them to yourself, but proclaim God's message, so His people may be prepared for His Second Coming. It is by faith that you speak out, and trust in Me that I will provide you what to say. Never doubt My love and speak out with authority, for I am guiding your speech. Give praise and glory to God for all He does through you."*

Later, at Adoration, I had a deep sense of the power of God throughout the universe. Then, I could see some men in a biosphere thinking they could live there on their own. Jesus said: *"My people, why are you so wrapped up in how great you think you know science and the art of survival? If you knew even twice what you know now, you would only be scratching the surface of all there is to know. When you are before My Blessed Sacrament, you are before My infinite love, which I wish to pour out on all who visit Me. I take your open hearts and I fill them with My graces and blessings. You are so fortunate to stand before your God and face the beauty of My power without having to know all of its effects by what you see. With the eyes of faith, you see a glow of My strength which men are too busy to stop and contemplate. Call on Me, My friends, at anytime for My help and I will seek to answer your prayer in the best way possible for your soul. Continue to give me praise and glory which my countenance calls all men to."*

Saturday, November 23, 1996:

After Communion, I could see chairs and tables all folded up and a large room was empty that was previously used for a Church. Jesus said: *"My people, I am showing you how your churches will be vacant as you will be prevented from openly worshipping me. A persecution of the church will rapidly escalate as the Antichrist's time arrives. You will then have to have your Masses in secret wherever a priest can be found. This will become harder as the priests will be sought out for persecution besides. You must have a good spiritual life of prayer to carry you through this time, so prepare now as the wise virgins secured oil for their lamps. Then, when I come in triumph, you will be ready to go forth into the wedding banquet of my victory."*

Later, I could see the end of a large pipe which carried many service lines for power, cable, and sewer lines. Jesus said: *"My people, your affluence has spoiled you with conveniences which have made you lazy and not fully appreciative of your blessings. Your advances in science have made your life easier than others. I tell you, it would be good for you to fast from the things you like and not just food. In that way you could show your control over things and not have them control you. At other times, do more for your fellow man out of love for Me. Help your neighbor who is in need and you will gain a friend and help Me in him. Look for ways in your life to do more suffering for My sake, so that you do not get so comfortable that you forget you are here to be tested in My love. Place more trust in My help than relying on your own ways to make ends meet. When you reach out more in faith to give Me all the glory and praise, you will get closer to perfection by following My plan for you."*

Sunday, November 24, 1996: (Christ the King)

After Communion, I could see Jesus at first in robes welcoming us. I then saw Him seated on a throne with a crown and He was holding a container full of stars indicating Him as the King of the Universe. Jesus said: *"My people, this is the end of the church year and this feast commemorates my Kingship not only over the earth, but over the universe as well. I am all loving, all merciful, all powerful, and all just. When you come before the foot of the altar, I am asking you to reverence My Blessed Sacrament, and give Me praise and glory for all I have done for you. This week is an excellent time to be thinking of giving thanks to Me as well. It is at the end of the church year that the readings talk about the end of your life on earth. The Gospel speaks of your final judgment before Me. I will truly separate the good on My right and the condemned at My left. It will be very much as in life. You are either with Me or against Me, there is no middle ground. If you wish to be with Me, then be the servant of the rest. You must reach out to help your neighbor in any way you can, but do it for love of Me as your motivation. I love all of you, but each person will be held accountable for their actions or inactions."*

Later, I could see several trains and subways going through tunnels. Jesus said: *"My friends, there are many tunnels for trains where hiding places could be found. As the time of the tribulation draws near, you may be led by your angels to such places, where the angels will provide space for you. During this trial, be thankful if you are kept alive, for many trials will test man's stamina in those days. Pray for My help which will be necessary to save your souls. As you see the dreaded evil agents of that time of the Antichrist, you will give thanks to Me for your protection. Even though evil will reign only a short time by your standards, it will seem like a living death for many. For those who are condemned, they will face a preview of the flames of hell on this earth. For those who are saved, some may face martyrdom, but others will live to see the new heaven on earth. This will be a reward for enduring the test of evil, and it will show you a little of what heaven will be like. Pray for the strength to endure this evil age, for many will be tested to the breaking point. I will watch over my faithful and I will send My angels to guard your souls from the evil ones."*

Monday, November 25, 1996:

After Communion, I could see Jesus in glory and He was holding forth a gleaming gold cup. Jesus said: *"My people, you are blessed that I did not pass up My cup of suffering for you on the cross. It is this same Body and Blood, I offer up for you at every Mass, so you may partake of Me, and I may come into your hearts and souls. Since you profess to be one of My disciples, all who accept Me and wish to be saved, must drink of this same cup of suffering. Each day that you start, requires its own suffering for you to get through your day. Seek My help every day in everything you do. Then you can offer up to Me as a prayer, all that you must put up with each day. Instead of complaining of your trials, when you offer them up, you will benefit from your own suffering. It is important what your intentions are, and if they*

are given up to Me, I will accept these sufferings as a down pay-
ment on your worthiness of being in heaven."

Later, at Our Lady of Lourdes I again could see an entrance to
a train tunnel. Jesus said: *"My son, I am showing you a similar*
vision to the day on which there was a train derailment. Because
of your news service, you are able to see so many events fall al-
most on top of one another. If you were noticing, you would see
how rapidly events are continuing, even now. Remember, I warned
you that events would speed up in the end times. If you are a
student of your own times, you would recognize these happen-
ings. You are indeed waiting for events that you would recognize

as more serious, and defined in My Scriptures. Have patience, for these times are arriving, but few of My faithful will understand these events. This is in keeping with My Scriptures, that the clever will be confused and the simple will have great understanding. It is not the proud or the rich who will inherit the earth, but My humble faithful who obediently follow My every wish. If you seek salvation in heaven, you must come to Me and give your will over to Me. When you let Me rule your life, then will the beauty of My understanding be made clear to you. Until you accept Me as Savior, you will never find your way to heaven. I am the resurrection and the life, no one can come to the Father unless they come through Me."

Tuesday, November 26, 1996:
After Communion, I could see a beaten up battle shield from battle. Jesus said: *"My friends, you are in the thick of battle for souls with the evil one. You have many signs of immorality and killings all around you. Were you to deny this era as evil, like Sodom and Gomorrah, you would be a liar. Again, you are without a doubt in the end times, since never before in your history, have you seen such events. You have seen an unparalleled increase in knowledge of science, more earthquakes than historical records show, many changes in your weather, famines in Africa and elsewhere, comets hitting Jupiter and many other omens in the sky. Again, if you think these are not the end times, you are sadly mistaken. My Second Coming is not far off, since My mother has warned you in many sites of apparition. Be forewarned about these signs, but most of all return to Me in confession, where I will forgive you your sins, so you can be spiritually prepared to do battle for your soul. Those who do not prepare, will be swept away in ruin like the man who built his house on sand."*

Wednesday, November 27, 1996:
After Communion, I could see snow being plowed and shovelled out of driveways. Jesus said: *"My people, it is indeed interesting from My vantage point to see how each person deals with testing and hardships in their lives. As you see this recent storm come, take a look at how some chose to deal with it. There are*

some who keep digging out in an attempt to keep ahead of future snow. Then others leave it go, and they have one huge pile to remove. You can look at your spiritual lives similarly. It is better to meet temptations and rid them first, instead of letting sin take over. Then if you should sin, it is better to immediately seek My grace of confession to clean your soul. If you let sin build up without any forgiveness in your heart, it becomes increasingly difficult to come back to Me by warming your cold hearts. This is why I encourage monthly confession to keep your soul plowed out of sin. Otherwise, you will meet an avalanche of sin and find it difficult to remove. Keep close to Me always and I will keep your home fires of love forever burning."

Later, at Adoration I could see a baby on an altar of what could have been a black mass. Jesus said: *"My son, you have come with heavy questions, but I have told you not to deny any of these messages. The Antichrist will have powers beyond that of a mere man. Many will ask how he came to have these powers. You are being shown that this man has been consecrated to evil beings to do his appointed task. You are right that he will have more power than a man, but he receives these powers through his initial offering to the demons. If you doubt these powers, read the Scriptures and see what they say about him. In all you do, you must be obedient to those acting in My place. Trust My priests, because of their gifts and follow their instruction. In this way you will take away any misunderstanding concerning the messages. You truly will have to avoid the Antichrist and his powers which will be strong during his brief reign."*

Thursday, November 28, 1996: (Thanksgiving Day)
After Communion, I could see a turkey and some food. Jesus said: *"My people, many of My feast days are secularized, and this for your country is one of them. You have been blessed with many of My gifts, so it is fitting that you come back as the cured leper to give Me thanks and glory. It is good that you are here at My Eucharistic table to share in My bread of life. This is real food, for you are sharing in My Body and Blood which are necessary for life in Me. As you come to My table, I wish that you would remember to thank Me every day of your life, for the many gifts*

of life that I give you each day. I am your God and the one who loves you at all times. Send Me your love daily and give Me thanks, honor and praise at all times, just as the saints and angels do. Thank Me continuously for loving you and providing you with all that you need in life. Many things you take for granted, but if you reflected even on your health, you would see reason to be thankful. By offering up your prayers and actions each day to Me, you can send Me the best thank you, you can give Me."

Friday, November 29, 1996:

After Communion, I could see a beautiful altar with a casket and a glass door on top. All at once, the dead person came to life and the door opened as the person came out. Jesus said: *"My son, what I am to tell you may be difficult to understand. I wish to explain to you about the first and second resurrections and the first and second deaths. All people have been appointed to die once because of the effects of original sin. The first death is for all those who have died up to the end of the tribulation. You are judged initially where your spirit must come to rest. The first resurrection is for all those whose spirits have been reunited with their glorified bodies. These people will live through the era of peace. The first death is also associated with the first judgment as well. At the end of the era of peace, I will come in final judgment. This will be the second resurrection as you will be brought with your glorified bodies into heaven for those who are saved. This time will be the second death for those accursed who will be reunited with their bodies and cast into hell for eternity or in the ever present now without time. Rejoice, My faithful, on that day for you will know all love and peace in heaven, when time will cease. You will then give Me constant praise and glory, for you will have reached perfection in all I created for you. Live on in faith, My children, so you can live with Me in this ecstasy of your spirit and body made whole."*

Later, I could see some parents swinging their kids followed by a scene of taking them to school. Jesus said: *"My people, many parents are very good at providing recreation and the proper schooling, but how many of these parents are as concerned with the spiritual lives of their children? It is even more important to teach them of the ways of faith than to have them brilliant in worldly knowledge. Many still have to learn that caring for their souls, is the most important task that all parents need to take care of, since their souls are immortal. That, which lasts forever, is more deserving of your attention than all that is passing away before you. Therefore, you parents should take extra time to teach your children their prayers and the truths of their faith. In that way, you may teach them that advancing in their faith, is more important than all the degrees they could obtain from the world."*

Saturday, November 30, 1996:

After Communion, I could see some Christmas lights and those that were ringing bells for contributions to the poor. Jesus said: *"My people, as you prepare for another Christmas season, your shopping for gifts becomes for some an obsession. Do not let your vigor for shopping lead you away from the true meaning of Christmas. Just as you saw these giving pots for the poor, think of whatever you can give to those less fortunate, who cannot repay thee. So when you see these reminders of charity, make a plan to help those who are truly needy. In helping them, you are like donating to the little Baby of Bethlehem. Whenever you help the least in My kingdom, you are helping Me."*

Later, I could see some tents where prisoners were being held in detention centers. Jesus said: *"My people, your time of testing draws near, but I will see to your protection wherever you will be. These agents of the Antichrist will have an agenda to eliminate many Christians and fighters for the faith. Many of my faithful will not fear being martyred for My Name's sake. Others will seek refuge at the save havens of My cross or the safe places the angels will lead you to. Some will be tested by starvation and diseases in the detention centers. It would be wise to avoid these centers, since many of them will be death camps. Listen to My warnings, so you will be able to go into hiding at a sudden notice. Many will be tested during this time, but when you give your suffering to Me, I will use it to mold you as examples of faith. It will be hard to keep the faith in those days, but look to Me and I will do the impossible for you. Believe in Me and I will see to your reward."*

Sunday, December 1, 1996:

After Communion, I could see a king's white robe laying on the ground and there were children all around. They were ready to celebrate Christmas, but there was darkness all around them. Jesus said: *"My people, it is important that you teach your children about the real meaning of Christmas. Do not build up their expectations of Christmas gifts from Santa Claus, such that they forget it is a feast day to celebrate My Birth and My Incarnation as a man. Also, teach them of My parents — Joseph and Mary. It is right to have them familiar with Scripture, which will show them the history of man, and how I became a part of it for love of man. Children are very impressionable, so it is important to bring them out of the darkness of the world's promises, and into the light of My love and My salvation. The earlier you teach them of My Presence, the sooner they can be thinking of their loving creator. My coming to your world will be further enhanced with My Second Coming, when all evil will be wiped away. So, when you are joyous around Christmas, be thinking to share that joy with Me and your children as well."*

Later, I could see flowers on the altar on the table with the Blessed Sacrament. In the next scene I could see a casket, but it was empty. Jesus said: *"My people, you are seeing these flowers before Me as an honor and praise to Me, but at the same time they are a thank you for all the prayers that were miraculously answered. The empty casket means that death was robbed and people are living thanks to healing prayers. Have faith in My healing powers and you will see your prayers answered. Many lose hope in the early going, but those who persevere in their prayers, I will answer them. Give your suffering over to Me, and I will turn it into a blessing. Continue to offer Me all your sufferings, physical and mental, each day and I will store these as heavenly treasures for the judgment. Pain can be used to make reparation for past sins. All you need to do is offer an intention with your prayer."*

Monday, December 2, 1996:

After Communion, I could see a stage turned upside down and there was a large audience. Jesus said: *"My people, I am turning the tables over on you once again. Once I chased out the money*

changers from My temple. In that day I told them that they had
to worship God and not the money they were so concerned about.
Again in your day, I am turning things upside down, since you
are worshipping everything but Me. If you spend more time with
sports, earning money, or shopping, you are placing more im-
portance on the things of this world than Me. If you are to save
yourselves with My help, you must make more time for Me, so I
will have an opportunity to come into your hearts. Start today to
make room for Me at the inn of your soul, and room for Me in
the manger of Bethlehem. In this way I may be the light of your
soul which will scatter the darkness of your sins."

Later, I could see a large audience in an auditorium and there
was a section of small children seated. Jesus said: *"My people, you*
must teach the children at all times to know the faith through
each parent. Many times I brought the children close to Me, even
while My apostles tried to keep them away from Me. They are
precious in My eyes, and their souls need to be watched over at
all times. Do not push them aside and ignore your duty to teach
them the faith and their prayers. You teach them constantly, even
by your actions, so be watchful if you are giving good example.
My children must be watched, if you are a parent, a grandparent,
or even a concerned relative or friend. You must help in bringing
up the next generation in faith, since you are the link in passing
on the traditions I have given My apostles. Think of how you
received your faith, and how important it was for you that a
teacher or a parent helped mold you in knowing your salvation is
with Me. This is why it is so important for you to be that special
someone to bring the faith to a child of mine. I call you to evan-
gelize at all times, especially to keep teaching the children about
My love for them."

Tuesday, December 3, 1996: (St. Francis Xavier)
After Communion, I could see some airplanes in an airport
loading passengers. Jesus said: *"My son, I am showing you, how*
you will be My missionary to bring My Word to My people. Your
country truly is a missionary land because your affluence has
caused many to spiritually go to sleep. My warning of My Second
Coming and the trial of the coming tribulation, needs to be told

to the people as fast as possible. You do not have the luxury of time, so spread My message as far as you can go. Call on the Holy Spirit in your speech, and your angels to protect you in your travels. I am asking My people to wake up at this time and ready themselves for the spiritual battle going on in front of you right now. It is the conversion of souls to Me which is so important at this time. Seek My forgiveness in confession, so that all of My faithful may have washed robes to meet Me at My Second Coming. Heed My words, My people, and you will be saved."
Note: I had some food stuck in my throat and I could not swallow.

Later, I could see down someone's throat. Then I saw some green trees and bushes as in normal life. Jesus said: *"My son, you are being tested in many ways, and some you do not even realize. In everything, you must suffer for My sake. Pray for My help and I will see you through every difficulty. Do not fear any problems, but see all things as a challenge to test your faith. People are easily upset by little inconveniences, but you must live every moment in My love and overlook them. Offer Me up every little suffering, so I can use it to satisfy the reparation for sin in your world. Think more how you can help me, than worrying over the little things in your life. Some of My children I am asking more suffering from, because I know they are willing to suffer for Me, as I suffered for you on the cross. Once you see what you can suffer and the good that it does, you would be more willing to suffer for Me also. I do not force My Will on you, but I let your love for Me lead you to follow Me. I love all of you, and I have a special place in My heart for all of My suffering servants."*

Wednesday, December 4, 1996:

At St. Charles after Communion I could see a beautiful well decorated corridor. Then I saw Jesus struggling to carry His cross as He fell to the ground. Jesus said: *"My dear son, I had to suffer much for the sins of this world. As you look to the saints, they also had to suffer, but look at the reward they were given. Your work is to help bring souls back to Me, but many times there is a price for these souls. So when you suffer in any way, offer it up for the souls being touched by the books and your spoken word. In everything you do and experience give glory and praise to God*

to carry on in His name. You will see many testings of varying severity, but keep your focus on Me and I will guide you to many souls that need conversion. There is not much time left, but the stakes are high for those you minister to. Pray and offer your suffering for the benefit of these sinners. Your heart will be warmed to see the fruit of your labors with My help. Dedicate your life to Me and follow me wherever I lead you."

Thursday, December 5, 1996:

After Communion, I could see a white glowing object as a soul going up into a setting sky. Jesus said: *"My people, your time here on earth is short, and you do not know when I will call you home. This is why many times I have warned you in the Scriptures to be on guard, for you know not the day of My return either. In either case of your death, or My Second Coming, it would be wise to have your soul in order, ever ready to meet your Maker at the judgment. I have advised you to seek My forgiveness frequently, at least once a month in confession. By keeping your soul clean, you will be ready should death suddenly knock on your door. You, yourself have met a close encounter, even in an innocent mishap of eating. Use this as an example for yourself and others that your life can be called from you at any time. I love all of My people, but you must honor and love your God to show your love for Me."*

Later, at the prayer group, I could see Mary come in white for the Immaculate Conception. Mary said: *"It is not just a coincidence that you are giving a talk on my feast day. You are bringing my same message of my Son's Second Coming. You also will be encouraging the people to pray my three Rosaries and the fasting on Wednesday and Friday. In all of these things, I have asked my children to pray for peace in your world and the conversion of sinners. Remember to continue your consecration prayers, since they will be a preparation for you at your talk. Give thanks to my Son and me for helping you in your mission."* I could see Mary coming as an ethereal shimmering white spirit. She was hovering over some crosses. Mary said: *"My dear children, use this Advent time as a means to prepare yourself to remember my Son's Coming as man into your world. He loves each of you so much that He came into this world for the sole purpose of liberating your souls by his death on the cross. This was a mission planned for many years, since God promised he would send a redeemer to earth. You have seen the fulfillment of His first promise. Soon you will witness His second promise, that He would come again to judge all of mankind."* I could see people getting out their Christmas decorations. Jesus said: *"My people, as you are getting your Christmas trees ready, think more of making My nativity scene of more significance. It is good to remember your old traditions of lighting your Advent wreaths. This is a good opportunity to unite your families in prayer at dinner time. Keep your prayers ever on your lips at all times, so I may be a part of your lives every day."* I could see a priest in his Sunday vestments and there were many empty seats in a large Church. Jesus said: *"My people, you have been concerned over not having enough priests for your sacraments. This has been a contrived shortage in many places, but it also is a result of not enough people praying for more priests. Encourage your sons who wish to take up a blessed calling. Do not stifle any possible vocations, but help them succeed in their mission. While priests are decreasing, there is a decrease also in the laity attending Mass. Do not let your work or worldly pursuits take you away from Mass. Your priorities are not following My Will if you use such excuses."* I could see some major fires at refineries and natural gas stations. Jesus said: *"My son, you are seeing such fires caused by arson to upset your infrastructures, as such events will be leading to a takeover in your country. Many unsettling incidents will be occurring, so a state of emergency will be declared. In this way, Satan's agents will begin his preparations for the Antichrist to gain control. Do not be surprised when you see these events come upon you. You will need to go into hiding as these events unfold."* I could see some crocodiles near the Nile and this signified a renewal of evil coming from Egypt. Jesus said: *"My people, I went into Egypt in flight from Herod, but I came out of Egypt to later begin My public life on earth. In these end days you will see the evil ones come up out of Egypt as well. The old gods worshipped there will be invoked once again. Look for these events as the Antichrist comes to power."* I could see a river in a cave and I came out into a bright light at the end of the tunnel. Jesus said: *"My people, My coming at Bethlehem is a light which has come to your world — a light of salvation in the darkness of your sin. Rejoice, for My coming into your world was a sign that My redemption is at hand. I have given you My Eucharist, so My grace and strength will go before you until I come again. You have My light with you daily, if you would come to My crib at daily Mass. I am here, ready to give you My blessings, if you would only come to receive them."*

Friday, December 6, 1996: (St. Nicholas)
After Communion, I could see a dark night with a large spider web on a large window. Then I saw the web broken and a light

went through the darkness. Jesus said: *"My people, as you see Me coming at Christmas, I come as the Light of the world to dispel the darkness of sin. As you have seen the devil's web shattered, I come to conquer sin and death. It is in Me that you are freed from your sins. I am offering you forgiveness and a chance to enter heaven. Heaven, once closed by the sin of one man, is now opened again by the God-man. It is My death and resurrection that sets you free. Still, you are the one who must decide to love Me or not. Heaven has been offered to you, but you must accept this gift by following My will. If you love Me and you want to be saved, you must show Me your love and the doors to heaven will be opened to you."*

Later, I could see the pope saying Mass and before him I could see many colors of all the flags of the world. Jesus said: *"My people, I have sent you Pope John Paul II as the pope for the end times. He represents Me on earth and he is living the message to go out and teach all nations. His faith is strong and resolute as the Holy Spirit guides what he is to say. He is My authority on earth and he guides My Church on the right path. Some have hesitated to recognize him as that authority, since they wish to follow their own agenda, which is not always in conformity with church teachings. I tell you, My pope is following My Will for you and you should listen and follow what he tells you. Many want to change the traditions of the church, but you should not listen to those who believe only in change for its own sake. My words are forever, and should not be changed or misinterpreted. Let Me guide you on your path to heaven, and do not waver by listening to today's false witnesses."*

Saturday, December 7, 1996:

At the Park Plaza Hotel in L.A., California, after Communion, I could see an Oriental setting that could have been from the Philippines. I saw a monstrance with the Blessed Sacrament and a brief picture of Mary behind the monstrance. Jesus said: *"My son, you are to be gracious to those who are receiving you. As you give your presentation, seek the help of My Holy Spirit in delivering My message to the people. Tell the people also of My unconditional love and the gift of My Presence in My Blessed Sacra-*

ment. You know of My graces and strength that I give you in Communion each day. Even though My warnings are hard to accept, you must still give the message that I have asked you to show the people. Show them also My hope and the trust they must have in My help. I love all of My people, and I pursue you to your dying day. It is up to you, My people, to decide to follow My Will. If you do follow My Will, you will be saved. Live daily in My love and I will see to your needs."

Sunday, December 8, 1996: (Immaculate Conception)

At St. Denis' Church, in Diamond Bar, California, after Communion, I could see a small window or circular picture frame and inside was a picture of Jesus wearing a crown of thorns. Next to Jesus was a picture of Mary sorrowing for her Son's suffering. Mary came and said: *"My dear son, I am thankful that you are celebrating my feast day, for it is fitting that you give your talk on this feast for your country. My Son, Jesus, has given you messages to prepare the people of your country. You have seen throughout your life how I have brought you to my Son, Jesus, especially at Medjugorje. Now, my Son, Jesus, and I are leading you forward, so you can show others how I lead sinners to my Son. Give your example of conversion to show them how I lead you to my Son. Now, in this Advent season show the people it is repentance that I call My children to in preparation for Christmas and my Son's Second Coming. Go forward now and preach the word my Spouse, the Holy Spirit, will help you to witness to Jesus."*

Later, at Fairflex, California, after Communion, I saw Our Lady in white walking by. Mary said: *"My son, I am thanking you for doing my Son, Jesus' work on my feast day. I am thanking you personally as your reward. Your words spoken through the Holy Spirit have touched many hearts. Your expression of faith will ignite love for my Son, Jesus with an even higher pitch. Your witness is sincere and humble. My Son, Jesus' message of the end times is difficult, yet hopeful at the same time. Learn a lesson from each talk you are giving, that you remain faithful to your mission and confident in the Holy Spirit's help. Continue ministering to my children in their need. Your faith and concern for souls is contagious and it will give example to others to evangelize. Continue to witness to my Son, Jesus and me and you will reap your rewards in heaven.*"

Monday, December 9, 1996: (Immaculate Conception celebrated) At Riverside, California, in St. Catherine of Alexandria Church, I could see a statue in an alcove representing Our Lady's birth. I then could see the San Francisco Bridge and other signs of our country and Mary came beautifully dressed with a crown in white and shimmering brightness. Mary said: *"My dear children of America, I come to you to encourage you to bow down to the glory of my Son. He is grieved over your many offenses before him. I beg you to pray for the stopping of your many abortions, where the guardian angels of these souls are calling for God's judgment. Pray, also, to stop your many sins of the flesh, and all the greed for money and possessions. In all you do, I want to help purify you, my children, for many have fallen asleep in their duties to the Lord. It is time for your country to wake up in its leaders and in its family values. Please listen to me, my children, and cleanse your sins. Do not embarrass me before my Son, Jesus. I wish you to become shining examples of love for Him, but you must work hard to rid the many sins of the world about you. Turn from evil and do good, that is my desire for all of you in America.*"

Later, at St. Francis de Sales, Adoration of the Blessed Sacrament, Riverside, CA, I could see a long horizontal opening and inside I could see a large cross with Jesus on it laying on the ground out of sight. Jesus said: *"My people, I wish to show you the significance of My suffering on the cross, because you yourselves will suffer in these end times. I am showing you this concealed cross, since the evil men will be encouraged by the demons to destroy all remembrances of Me. They do not want men to be saved, so they will destroy all religious objects and forbid them to be made or possessed. This is why you must buy and store many rosaries and blessed religious objects now, so you can take them with you to flee the clutches of these evil men. These are your weapons to fight evil. Do not take any guns or anything destructive. Carry My cross with the corpus, so I can protect you through your weapons of My mercy. Prepare now, My people, since your time is short before you will face this time of tribulation. I will watch over you and protect you, but pray for My intervention and I will fly to your aid."*

Tuesday, December 10, 1996:
After Communion, I could see a large shooting star and then the surface of the earth was aglow with fire from volcanoes. Jesus said: *"My people, have faith and be patient, for not much longer and you will see the prophecies of Isaiah will be fulfilled. Recognize the signs of the end times that are around you. Those who believe things will continue on as they are, will be suddenly shaken. I will be a shepherd guarding My flock through the coming tribulation. Soon you will see the mountains made low and paths made straight as I will renew the earth to its former glory. Rejoice, My faithful, for My victory is close at hand. Then all that was told you about Me, will come about, as I bring My faithful to heaven on earth, when I come on the clouds to judge all mankind."*

Later, I could see a picture of the Pope on a tapestry. I then could look down a long spiraling staircase. Jesus said: *"My people, look to My Pope John Paul II for your support in My love. He is the one showing you My example by all he is suffering. Many have struggles of their own and they have to carry their cross in life. Each person is given a cross especially crafted by Me. Your crosses are special and you need to take them up every day and give them back to Me as a prayer. You all have been given graces to handle whatever I give you. Have confidence in My comfort and My protection. For those who take the yoke of My light burden on their shoulders, I will give them My rest and My love. Seek Me and I will show you the way to solve all of your problems."*

Wednesday, December 11, 1996:
After Communion, I could see my pastor, Fr. Jack dressed in his priestly vestments. Jesus said: *"My people, pray for your priests, especially the priest who administers the sacraments to you. Since they are fewer in number, pray for their strength to be uplifted, so they can carry out their demanding schedules. Help them in every way, that you may help lighten their burdens and give your support in every way. Lift them up to Me as you realize the beau-*

tiful service they provide in bringing Me to you. They need much support and it is your duty that you may help them to continue running their parishes. Pray also that the Harvest Master may send you more priests, so the faithful may be served in their needs."

Thursday, December 12, 1996: (Our Lady of Guadeloupe)
After Communion, I could see Maria E. vaguely at first and then strongly for a minute. I then saw Mary first as Our Lady of Fatima and then as Our Lady of Guadeloupe. Mary said: "*My dear children, you are seeing other places where I have performed miracles to demonstrate for you and enhance your faith in all the people in my visitations. I am coming in many ways to bring you to my Son. As you know, many conversions of Indians occurred after this vision and most of all them stopped killing the infants in worship to their gods. Today, many infants are being killed also in worship of your almighty dollar or your convenience. Those seeking abortions should have thought more of their actions, if they could not take care of their children. Think more closely that many of your problems are of your own making. Pray, my children, to imitate me and my Son and you will have no worries or fears, but only love for God and neighbor. Remove this sin of abortion from your land and many of your chastisements will be lessened.*"

Later, at the prayer group, I could see from behind a man's head and gradually the vision showed a large audience and I was at the head talking. Jesus said: "*My son, I have asked you to spread My Word at every opportunity that I have provided for you. Thank you for listening to My call, as I am leading you forward to speak in many places of My Second Coming. Your messages that I give you, are powerful, so speak them with My authority. In a word shout them from the rooftops, so My faithful may heed My words and be saved.*" I could see Mary and there was a brilliance which shined out from her in all directions. Mary was with child, much like in the image of Guadeloupe. Mary said: "*My dear children, I come as the woman dressed in the sun, about to give birth to my Son as you remember Jesus at Christmas. Pray, my children, for you have many problems in your world that can only be healed by prayer. I thank you for the flood of your Rosaries, that I will put toward your intentions and mine. Continue to keep your prayers coming in a steady stream, especially to stop your sins of abortion. I have told you, if enough prayers come forward, I will conquer your abortion mortuaries.*" I could see an old arch and a stained glass window in an old Church. Jesus said: "*My people, protect and preserve My Remnant Church. My Church is where My priests offer the Holy Sacrifice of the Mass with My people. Wherever My consecrated Host is present, I am there in your midst. Keep My Mass and My Blessed Sacrament sacred and guard it from being desecrated. There is coming a trial when you will need to offer Mass in secret. Do whatever is necessary to hold on to your traditions and imitate My Words in the Scripture.*" I could see a cross and then a picture of Pope John Paul II was seen behind the cross. Jesus said: "*My people, my pope son is suffering his cross with you. Many will be pressing in on him in these times. His strength will be tested as he leads My people along their pilgrimage with their own crosses. Pray for him, since he needs your many prayers to carry on. Listen to My pope son and follow his every word, since the Holy Spirit speaks through him.*" I could see St. Therese come with red roses and she was looking on a statue of Mary. St. Therese said: "*My son, I wish to draw your attention to the many red roses that were found on Juan Diego's tilma during the winter. Remember my love for flowers as signs for you on this beautiful feast of the blessed mother. Call her children to send their flowers of their Rosaries to be given to Mary, so she can take them to her Son. You have many abortions in your land. Send these red roses of your love in your prayers to stop this abomination. Make every rose remind you of every life that is taken. I am asking people to save souls, and start by saving the souls of these mothers seeking abortions. Stand up for these aborted souls and protect them.*" I could see a nun dressed in black and it appeared as Blessed Faustina. She said: "*Listen to my call for doing the Chaplet of Divine Mercy. These prayers are given to you to reverence Jesus as your Savior and remember his loving death on the cross for you. Come forward to follow the Divine Will as I have given you an example. Live to give every day over to Jesus and you will perfect your lives by following his plan for you. I love you all, my children, live the messages that I have shown you by my life.*" I could see some crowns falling to the ground, and many gold chairs were falling backwards. Jesus said: "*My people, you will see many of the leaders of your nations falling from their places of power. As the Antichrist comes at the tribulation, he will assume full authority over all the nations. He will be allowed a length of time in history to test man. I will be with you at that time protecting you, but your faith must be strong at that time. I will allow My mother to crush the head of Satan with her foot as our triumphs over him will soon come to pass. Rejoice, all of mankind, for your Lord will come in glory thereafter.*"

Friday, December 13, 1996: (St. Lucy)

After Communion, I could see a wallet laying on the ground at night. Jesus said: "*My people, how many times have I told you, you must die to yourself, or you cannot be My disciple? For many, their wallet is their god and their life. You cannot live for money and have a viable spiritual life. Do not let the cares and pleasures of life choke you to a spiritual death. The soul strives to be with Me, so do not let your desire for money or anything else hold you as a prisoner. I have come on the cross to set you free of your sins. So loose the bonds of the world and your money and follow Me first. When you seek My will, all that you need will be provided for you. See where real value is in My words of eternal life. Follow My road to heaven and I will shower you with the riches of My heavenly gifts which will last forever with Me.*"

Later, I saw a large hill and a rainbow was arched over the hill. On the hill I saw many crosses standing up with people on them. Jesus said: "*My people, learn from this vision that you must hang on hope and trust in Me, no matter what crosses you encounter. See that you pray to Me often to help guide you along the path of your life. See also, that no matter how hard you try to do things on your own without Me, that you will continue to fall on your face in failure. Learn that the only successes you have, will come to you, but not by your own skills, but by My grace in My gifts. All that you have has come through My gifts to you. All that you have, can be taken from you at anytime. Once you realize how life repeats this theme, you will see that it is better to go along with My will, than depend on the pride of your own efforts. Follow your own will, and you will not be in harmony with Me. All those who refuse Me, meet eventually with My justice and their own failures. See, therefore, it is I that your soul should seek, and My Will that is what will lead you to heaven. All other paths lead to hell and many find their fate in this way."*

Saturday, December 14, 1996:

At Christ the King Church, Atlanta, Ga., before the Blessed Sacrament, I could see an icon of Mary holding Jesus and they were seated on a throne and they were wearing crowns. They were pictured ornately in silver and gold. Jesus said: *"My people, I am showing you how closely our two hearts are joined together. My mother, Mary, is a very significant part of Advent and Christmas, since it was her consent that initiated the events for My Coming into the world. You all know how much I favor My mother, and how I answer many prayers asked of Me through her. You are celebrating My kingship at Christmas, since I promised you a redeemer throughout the centuries. See also, My mother has been very involved in announcing My Second Coming as well. Now, My son, I am preparing you once again to bring My Word to My people. Show them how My love overwhelms them, so they are drawn to Me out of sheer joy and a desire to serve. I ask all of you to follow Me as I asked My apostles. Have no fear and I will lead you in ways you could not dream of. Have faith and trust in Me, My people, for soon you will share in My renewed kingdom, with My victory over Satan."*

Sunday, December 15, 1996:

At Christ the King Church, Atlanta, Ga. at adoration I could see cars and bridges and people were moving fast both in their pace of life and in driving on the road. All at once I was taken to a place of peace and quiet. Jesus said: *"My people, your style of living has forced you in many ways to live at a faster pace than is necessary. You have grown accustomed to so many comforts, that these earthly things influence your thinking more than My love desires you to follow. When you are before My Blessed Sacrament, My peace slows you down and gives you a chance to exam-*

ine your life's priorities. It is when you stop to listen to My advice to you, that you learn the true values of life. Do not be so concerned with gaining more wealth in this world just to have more comforts. Your incentives should be to do things for Me, instead of following your own selfish desires. Let this be a guideline for you in your decision making. Think of what is important in life. Your spiritual life should far outweigh your bodily needs. Direct your life to storing up heavenly treasures by serving Me and your neighbor. When you serve only your self, you are being misdirected by the evil one. Stay close to Me and put Me first in your life, then you will be following My will and My plan for you."

Later, at St. John Christosdom Church, Atlanta, Ga., after Communion, I could see a priest in ornate vestments meeting with another priest in vestments. They were shaking hands. Jesus said: *"My people, I am showing you another sign of the end times, when My eastern and western churches will be united as one. My pope son has made overtures to the eastern churches. My children are both adoring Me in different ways, but you are so close to Me in spirit. See that many divisions in the churches are like the Tower of Babel in languages. Man with his pride has caused these divisions, but I never intended it to be so. Come close to Me in My love and you will see that I am the same Jesus for all of my people who wish to accept Me as Lord over their lives."*

Monday, December 16, 1996:

After Communion, I could see some stars or comets in the sky as the Book of Numbers talked of a star in the readings. Jesus said: *"My people, My Star of Bethlehem was foretold as I came forth from the line of David. My kingdom was announced by the star coming forward. The three kings of the orient give witness to My kingdom. Soon, you will see another sign in the heavens announcing the Antichrist's reign. Be attentive to the signs around you and understand how prophecy is foretold. I will be watching over My people at all times. Have faith, My people, for I am at you side to defend you from the ravages of the demons and the Antichrist."*

Later, at Our Lady of Lourdes I could see a glass chandelier and it was in the shape of a tear drop. Jesus said: *"My people, I am crying many tears for you, and I am still suffering on the cross for your frequent sins. I am crying because you commit the same sins over and over with no remorse for your offenses. What am I to do with you, my people? I call you to repentance through many messages of My messengers, but still you will not listen. My people, it is very important that you practice monthly confession. Without contrition for your sins, they will never be forgiven. Come to me in this sacrament of reconciliation with your tears of sorrow to show Me that you really care that your sins offend Me. I await you always to grant you forgiveness, but you must make the first step to restore this love bond which is broken by your sins. I am willing to heap many blessings upon you, if you would only wake up and come forward in contrition of your sins. Once your sins are forgiven, I will lift you up in the glory of My graces and you will love Me more than anything else in your world. Come to Me, My children, My love beckons you to place My light in your souls and fill them up with a measure of My Holy Spirit."*

Tuesday, December 17, 1996: (Genealogy of Jesus)

After Communion, I could see a vision looking down on the Dome of the Rock Temple in Jerusalem. Jesus said: *"My people, for the Jewish people the links to the great fathers of faith were very important. Since, I am the God-man promised by the Scriptures, it is important also, to see the many links throughout the history of mankind. My power as King is shown throughout all these generations, so that you can see how I have a plan for man and I mold him according to My will. Even to this generation you have links to the past by your birth in the effects of original sin. I have come to redeem all of mankind, so that My promise of salvation can be offered to all. Come to me, My people, so you can rejoice at the commemoration of My birth."*

Later, I could see people playing baseball and there was a backstop, but it had a hole at the middle from being used a lot. The ball as a result would pass through the screen. Jesus said: *"My people, when something loses its usefulness, it is ready to be cut down and thrown into the fire. It is as I told you about the salt when it looses its flavor and it becomes useless to season the earth. This also is true of your faithfulness to Me. If a person looses their connection to God, they have lost their natural calling to a higher being for their direction. Do not wander aimlessly and be distracted from My love and My plan for you. Look beyond yourself to where you are going. Life is too short to be lost in the darkness of your sins. Wake up and see My light is calling you home to be with Me in heaven. See the duties I call on each of you to perform. When you do them, you are doing nothing more than what is expected of one of My creatures. Come to Me and receive the fulfillment of your destiny of serving Me to gain heaven."*

Wednesday, December 18, 1996:
    After Communion, I could look through a keyhole and see Jesus in the manger as an infant. Jesus said: *"My people, I am knocking on the doors of your hearts to let Me in. Many of you are shopping and preparing for Christmas presents. Please do not rush around so much that you forget to let your Master come into your hearts. My love cries out for you, but many have turned your backs on Me and there again is no room for Me at the inn. There is love and care awaiting you in My manger. Take the time to let Me in to your hearts and I will warm your soul with a deep emotional flood of graces and blessings. I am the one to heal all of your problems, if you would just give them over to Me. I am delighted when you come to Me, but do not wait so long, such that your hearts grow cold to Me. This is a joyous season and I wish to share My love with all of those who wish to visit Me at my crib."*

Thursday, December 19, 1996:
    At the prayer group, I could see a tabernacle and it opened by itself. I then looked up and I could see Jesus coming on a cloud in glory to judge the people of this age. Jesus said: *"My people, you are witnessing my Second Coming when I will come upon the clouds and claim triumph over Satan and all evil. From that time on, I will be with My faithful in a special presence when no longer will you require My sacraments to receive Me. This will be the time when I will cast the demons and all the evil men into the pool of fire. Those unworthy will not be a part of My era of peace. Come to Me now, My people, and prepare for this spiritual battle."* I could see a large dark wall placed in front of a well lighted Nativity scene. Jesus said: *"My people, why do the people push aside*

My nativity scene, so that it no longer can be found in public? Christmas is the celebration of My birth, but people are afraid to display Me in public. Remember Me especially, in your homes by this scene. Keep in mind what you are celebrating, so you can welcome Me into your hearts. Come with your rosaries tonight to commemorate this Mystery of the Rosary in the Nativity." I could see an outline of a Christmas tree and then a very red sky behind. There was a silhouette of people carrying many weapons. Jesus said: *"My people, I come at Christmas to bring peace on earth and good will to men, but still there are remnants of the red tide of communism ready to unleash a new attack on the world. These former powers lie dormant, but are ready to renew their hopes to control the world. In your prayers continue to pray for My peace that men will cease their fighting and come to Me in love."* I could see Mary come and she was showing me this sign in the window of her presence. Mary said: *"My dear children, many times you are amazed at the signs from heaven. I have come in many places of apparition to witness my Son's Second Coming. All of these happenings are signs for you to witness your faith to my Son. Come to His crib as I am forever leading you to Him."* I could see some headlights on an old car at night. Jesus said: *"My people, I am trying to show you that you should shed some light on your traditions of faith. Many doctrines of the church must be upheld and preserved so the gift of faith can be handed down to future generations. Hold dear to your heart the truths of your faith and do not be afraid to proclaim them in public, if you are asked to witness to them. Many evils in your society want to keep even My Commandments out of sight, because their guilt repels them from My Word."* I could see some fences of barbed wire and a train of large freight cars. Jesus said: *"My people, even though there are beautiful scenes and songs on My feast of Christmas, do not forget that to be a Christian, you will also be asked to suffer. Right after Christmas you celebrate many martyrs, so you do not get complacent that this is only a momentary joyful time. You will see a time coming where many will have to suffer for My Name. You will be tortured and some martyred in this coming tribulation. I come to protect your souls from the evil ones, so have no fear of them. With Me at your side, who can stand against you?"* I could see a car wrecked and off the road into a bush. Jesus said: *"My people, you see riots in your streets and many of your houses and buildings will be destroyed. You will see many shortages in food and fuel that will drive people to stealing and pillaging for survival. It is during this major unrest that the Antichrist will try to establish his peace. Do not believe his words, but go into hiding as I have warned you in many of My messages. Pray to Me and My angels to lead you to safety. Keep faith in My help and I will protect you."*

Friday, December 20, 1996:
After Communion, I could see a priest give Holy Communion to Maria E. I then could see a night scene where a dead body was placed in the water. Jesus said: *"My people, I detest this senseless and thoughtless killing of innocent lives. Those, who do these killings, try to hide their wrong doings, but one day they will be found out. Even if they are not punished in this life, surely I see all such evil and My justice will come swiftly over them. The taking of life, I have told you, is the most serious sin in any of its forms. Those, who do such things, will pay a heavy burden for denying My plan for their lives. Even such crimes can be forgiven, if these people come forward in confession. Woe unto them who do such things without repenting, for they truly will be punished in the flames of hell for all eternity."*

Later, I could see a bottle of alcohol come forward out from under a rug. Jesus said: *"My people, I am asking you to be careful in any of your self-indulgences. Many times people wish to forget their troubles, and rely on drugs or drink to find some satisfaction. Each time you abuse your body in dulling your senses, you are left in a worse state of dependence. Do not look for artificial ways to avoid your problems. They will still be there, and now you will have worse problems of addiction. You can have dependencies on drugs, alcohol, cigarettes, or as you have seen even with computers. Do not let things control you, because you like to satisfy your selfish desires. Instead, give your troubles over to Me, and I will lead you through them. Many times you need to suffer to gain any grace or move ahead in your spiritual progress. By giving up your own desires in order to serve Me, you will see life from a completely different vantage point. By looking beyond the desires of the body, you will see the plan I call for your soul to come and follow Me. As your spiritual life is enhanced, you can then help others to come to Me through your evangelical efforts."*

Saturday, December 21, 1996:

After Communion, I could see some poor people collecting wood for a fire. Jesus said: *"My people, as you prepare your gifts for each other on Christmas, think of the poor who have no one to give them gifts. If you could help these poor little ones of mine, you would be bringing the best gift you could to My crib. Every little sacrifice you make for Me, is storing up heavenly treasure for when I come for you. See to it that you build up your treasure in heaven, than any vain treasure on earth. Your treasures on earth will disappear quickly, but those in heaven will be everlasting. Strive to serve Me in any way you can, and your rewards will multiply your efforts a hundredfold."*

Later, I was traveling down a street at a fast speed. The further I traveled down the street, the older the events went back in years. This happening seemed to describe the life review of the warning. Jesus said: *"My people, you know time is running out before the tribulation when you see the signs of My warning coming upon you. This will be a moment of truth for many, since they will have to choose between the pleasures of the earth or serving Me. Choose the way of heaven, My children, or a worse fate than persecution will befall you. Those, who turn away from My grace of mercy in the warning, will receive the worst condemnation, since they will see how to be saved and will have refused it. Take advantage of My mercy and come to Me in confession, so you can set your spiritual house in order to receive Me. My warning is coming soon, so heed My message and prepare for the coming purification. You will have many trials, but in the end you will prevail with My triumph over evil."*

Sunday, December 22, 1996:

After Communion, I could see a large crowd of people at Mass and the words *"...round yon virgin..."* could be heard. Our Lady came as she was about to give birth. Mary said: *"My dear children, you are seeing Me come as the Ark of the Covenant. God's First Covenant was given to Moses in the Ten Commandments and they were held in the Ark which traveled with the chosen people. Now, my Son's Second Covenant is fulfilled in his coming to earth and I carried Him in the new Ark of the Covenant. Come to greet my Son and bring Him your special offerings as did the three kings. Jesus brings you His peace and love. Accept Him into your hearts and your soul will be fulfilled with His Presence."*

Later, I could see some blue lines of weather patterns and they were influenced by electromagnetic radiation. Jesus said: *"My people, I have warned you about the severity of this winter, but I have not stressed how this will come to be. You will notice the effects of weather making Tesla machines on both the eastern and western seaboards. The powers of the one world government have no concern for the people of your country. They mean to use these storms that they are creating, to cause havoc in your country, so that when you are most vulnerable, they will seize an opportunity for takeover. Your president and the leaders of the world are planning a coup to assume global takeover in readiness for the Antichrist's coming. It is only a matter of time until they will strike down your constitutional rights in favor of a UN controlled government. Many forces are in position today, to assume power over the masses. Once the electronic chips are in place among the people, it will give them total control. Refuse to use these chips, My children, and they will not control you. They will torture you, but only those taking the chips will lose their spiritual souls to the nether world. Preach as long as you can, never to submit to Satan's power in these chips. I will be with you to the end."*

Monday, December 23, 1996:

After Communion, I could see an A and Ω carved out of clay or stone before me in a vision. Jesus said: *"My people, I am truly the beginning and the end of all life and all things that exist. There is no other to give praise and glory to except the one true God who rules over everything. When you consider the awesomeness of the power of your God, how could you give anything or any other being your allegiance? Your Creator calls to you everyday that you give Me thanks and glory for all the gifts I send you. Keep your mind free of all entanglements from the world. Keep your mind and heart focused on Me at all times, especially in remembering My commemoration of my birth on Christmas. I love all of my Children and I am concerned for souls to come to Me. I watch over each of you and I draw you to love Me as well."*

Note: A light was shining on the Blessed Sacrament and kept blinking with varying intensities.

Later, I could see great signs in the skies that were very dramatic and showing the sign of Antichrist's coming. Jesus said: *"My people, you have been given many signs and wonders of My end times among you. Still many fail to believe and they are trying to explain away their significance. I tell those doubters, you will soon see a series of events which can only be described as supernatural. All will see for themselves in my warning, how sin offends Me. You will then see destruction and chaos that have yet to occur in such rapid succession. The famine, plagues, and pestilence will announce the coming of the Antichrist. You will see great omens in the sky and the evil one will manifest many miraculous powers. When these things come to pass, many will be in fright of such events. There will be no doubt of these being the end times. Awaken, My faithful, and pray for My protection in these times, for without Me, everything would be hopeless. Follow My angels and fight the battle of good and evil. Do not give up, but rely on My strength to overcome this evil. This power of evil will last but a moment, when I will bring the victory through My triumph. Fear not, My people, but hold close to Me and I will protect you."*

Tuesday, December 24, 1996:

After Communion, I could see some kingly robes. Jesus said: *"My people, you have read of my lineage to King David. You have seen the three kings give me homage. At the end of My life, you have seen them mock me as King of the Jews. So you see My kingly robes now witness to My true Kingship as King of the Universe. I am the Son of God made man, so on entry into the world, I could be a ransom for all of your sins. Without My sacrifice, man would still be hopelessly lost in his sins. Rejoice, today, for this commemorates the lifting of your bondage from sin.*

You must come to Me at the crib and give homage to your Savior. Unless you acknowledge Me before men, I will not acknowledge you before My Father. Let My peace and joy settle in your hearts, as you celebrate this feast of My First Coming."

Later, after Communion at Midnight Mass, I could see Jesus coming down the aisle of a large crowd. Jesus said: *"My people, you have seen Biblical prophesy of My First Coming that has come to fruition in every detail. My public ministry required that I go before the people and preach to them the Good News of their Salvation. I went forward even in the face of danger in spreading the Word of My Father. So it is with My messengers who must go forward as I did, and preach My message of mercy and justice. You too, may face dangers to spread My Word, but you are in a battle of good and evil where you must witness to My power over any other evil force. Those who witness in My Name will reap a prophet's reward. Continue to teach the people to seek forgiveness of their sins and you will help many to be saved. If you do not do My work, you will have the guilt of not having saved those souls you could have touched. Accept My Will for you and continue to struggle in living My message day after day, that you will live according to My Will."*

Wednesday, December 25, 1996: (Christmas Day)

After Communion, I could see Jesus come in the clouds dressed in robes with a bright light coming from Him. Jesus said: *"See, My people, how glorious My Coming to you has been. Before I came, men were hopelessly lost in their sin. Now that I am with you, salvation is possible even for the worst of sinners. Give thanks and praise to Me for coming to earth as a man. You have been given witness in the Scriptures of My being and you have an example through My teaching of what is expected of you. You cannot deny My existence, therefore, nor can you deny the path to heaven I am leading you to. You can deny Me and not accept Me, but you know the punishment if you refuse Me. Come to My crib in faith today and receive your innocence back again as I forgive you your sins."*

Thursday, December 26, 1996: (St. Stephen)

After Communion, I could see a white hill outside of town as the type of place they stoned St. Stephen. Jesus said: *"My children, you may have great fervor for the faith and be well adept at evangelizing My Word, but still there will be unbelievers without the grace of faith to understand about Me. Pray for your persecutors to see the light one day, for in your day you will see these same pagans scoff and hurl threats at you because of My Name. They actually fear your words of love of God, because it threatens their pleasures of the world. Those in darkness of their sin refuse My saving grace and desire temporary comfort over the unknown spiritual eternity. Pray for these in earnest, for they are far from Me, and do not know of their destiny for the flames of hell if they do not change their lives. Men persecuted Me in My day and they will do no less in your time as well. Prepare for this coming purification, so you will be ready to suffer for Me in whatever I ask of you."*

Later, at the prayer group, I could see an outline in light of Our Lady as she was holding her mantle over some children. Mary said: *"My dear children, you remember the Scripture passage '...and Rachel was weeping for her children because they are no more.' You are approaching the feast of those Holy Innocents that died at the hands of Herod. Now, in your own world, innocent life is still being taken by abortion, but you mothers are not weeping for the loss of your children. Wake up to see the blood on your hands and pray to stop this ruthless killing of babies. Life is too precious to snuff it out with no regard. Pray for these mothers to stop killing their babies."* I could see an angel marking the names of those saved in the Book of Life. Jesus said: *"My people, My angels are walking among you. As they place My mark on the foreheads of My faithful, another angel records their name in My Book of Life. Come to Me now and be saved by My grace of forgiveness. Those, who see the light, give witness to the truth of My Words. Receive Me into your hearts, so I may send you My grace of protection in the coming tribulation."* I could see people storing food away for the time of the coming famine. Jesus said: *"My people, many have heeded My words on faith to store some food away for the coming famine. There are still many who do not believe, nor want to believe such a famine is coming. Do not depend on your media for such information, since your news is controlled by the same forces who are contriving this shortage. Look at the crop failures and prices if you doubt My word. Do not wait too long or you may have to suffer want in your own household. My words are not mocked, look to the Scriptures for what will be coming. My word will be fulfilled, if you want to believe it or not.*" I could see an old covered wagon to carry one's belongings when people moved out West. Jesus said: "*My people, I have asked you to prepare for the coming tribulation, both physically and spiritually. Pray for My strength to endure those days and be frugal in preparing your things to take with you. Have your spiritual weapons of rosaries, scapulars, crosses and holy water ready to take with you at a moment's notice. Have warm blankets and sweaters to carry as well. I give you warning, now that the time of your visitation draws near.*" I could see beautiful sights of Christmas cheer among the people. Jesus said: "*My people, My peace and love are showered down on you at this time. Many are helping others in need as the spirit of this Christmas season touches many hearts. Share your love and good will with those who may have sorrow or loneliness in their lives. A kind word is contagious and you can help many with your joy of faith. Bring My peace to all you can, so the grace of Christmas may shine on all peoples like My star over Bethlehem.*" I could see a track or conveyor belt of a mechanized carrying device. Jesus said: "*My people, you have grown accustomed to many time saving devices, but do not let them control your life. The more you become dependent on your electronic devices, the more your life is being controlled. Seek Me first in the simplicity of My call, and not the call of the world to the newest gadgets to possess.*" I could see some small children and their faces were beaming with love. Jesus said: "*My children, when you look into the eyes of your children, you see an innocence that is quickly corrupted with age and exposure to evil. As you look upon Me in my crib, give Me your love, and hold Me close, so you may not be one of My lambs who strays away from Me. Stay close to your Shepherd and I will protect you from the wolves who come as demons to taunt you. Pray often, My loving children, and I will guide you away from temptations that try to steal away your soul.*"

Friday, December 27, 1996: (St. John the Evangelist)

After Communion, I could see St. John at the foot of the cross. Jesus said: "*My son, I have entrusted an important message for you to deliver to My people at this time. Do not be concerned about the details of this gift, but see the gift of this blessing as being directed at saving souls for Me. You have seen how much St. John loved Me in all of his writings. Go, My son, and witness to the people of my love and protection, which I wish to shower on My faithful even now. Share My divine love with all who will listen to these messages. I am a God of constant love and mercy. Be faithful to your calling and abide by your prayer life to uphold your mission. Those, who are called now, have a heavy responsibility to spread My Word. Seek the power of the Holy Spirit in all of your public presentations."*

Later, I could see some black helicopter gunships as the one world forces were obtaining more sophisticated weaponry. Jesus said: *"My people, do not be surprised that the evil one will use all available technology for his mission. Many helicopters are being placed in position for crowd control near all the big cities. You will see, My children, how ruthless the evil ones can be when they decide to seek global control. These people will ready everyone to be under the control of the Antichrist. What you have seen up to now, will pale in the face of these evil forces soon to take over your countries and your cities. These things are being told you, not to frighten the people, but they are being shown to you, so you know what you will be dealing with in preparation for the tribulation. I keep telling you, that no one will survive without My help. You are right about the many confirmations that I have given you. Those, who refuse to prepare for this battle with evil, will be found wanting and unprepared. It would be better for you to be spiritually prepared, since you will need all of your spiritual weapons, as the rosary, to fight this battle. Continue to warn the people of these physical traumas, but most of all prepare to guard your souls which are the most valuable."*

Saturday, December 28, 1996: (Holy Innocents, Holy Family Mass)
After Communion, I could see a donkey. Later, I could see a donkey carrying Jesus in Mary before birth. Then I saw Jesus on the donkey going up to Jerusalem as on Palm Sunday. Jesus said: *"My people, I am showing an image of a donkey because there is a link between My Coming at Bethlehem and My going up to Jerusalem. I have come into this world to die for all the sins of mankind. In the first vision you see Me coming in My mother on a donkey as she was to give birth. In the second vision you are seeing Me going to Jerusalem on a donkey again, to face My passion and death. See also, that I was born into a loving family that gives you models for all members. You can see a father's role in My foster father, St. Joseph and a mother's role in My beautiful mother, Mary. It is important that you use the Holy Family as a model for your society. Many attacks come against the family, but you must pray together to hold families strong in this evil age."*

Later, I could see some people through prison bars. Jesus said: *"My people, some have taken on extra suffering for My name in defending My little ones. You have a depraved justice system that makes preferences into unnatural laws without even voting on them in legislation. When a nation's laws allow divorces, abortions and unnatural families, you are making men obey laws which violate My laws. You must see that divine laws demand your allegiance over and above any of man's false laws. When you are protesting these abuses in your society, you are following My wishes for true values to be upheld in life. You will see more and more inhumane laws come over you as this evil age tries to swallow up all goodness I have created. Continue to fight for the precious life I freely give to all mankind. Protect all life from this evil lust for death and killing. My justice will come shortly, to cast all this evil lot into the eternal flames of their punishment. Your sins are overflowing and My purification must cleanse the earth of all these treacherous deeds. Did you not think I would hold these men accountable for their actions? I will come indeed, to stop the evil which is causing Me to suffer continuously. All will be made new according to my will."*

Sunday, December 29, 1996: (Holy Family Sunday)
After Communion, I could see a family kneeling at Mass on Sunday. Jesus said: *"My people, it is important this day that you give reverence to the family as an institution, since I have used this imagery to show you how I am the groom and My Church is My spouse. In the Old Testament you have read 'I have made them male and female so that what I have joined together, let no man tear asunder.' in the New Testament also, I have shown those who believe, that it becomes adultery for each of those married who live with someone else even in divorce. I am quoting these passages, so you reverence the family in the tradition I have given it to you. Again, you have the example of My Holy Family as your model. The problem is that your society has not enforced its traditions and has been too permissive in its behavior. Divorce is the scourge of your society and it is the main reason for many of your troubles. When a people turns their back on God's laws, you will reap the harvest of your own destruction. Many societies*

have fallen apart more from within than from outside. Those, who accept this state of irreverence for the family, are teaching the wrong message. You should build up marriages and stop breaking them up because of your simple bodily desires and conveniences. You should abide by your commitments and treasure the marriage bond as your station in life. You have responsibilities to your spouses, your children and Me. Do not treat them lightly, but preserve the family values that have held societies together for years when followed. When you allow divorce and disrespect for Sunday by working, you are planting the seeds for the fall of America. As you see this evil age destroy your traditions, this is why your country is in its death throes."

Later, I saw a car riding on a road about to get on a ramp when suddenly there was someone in black riding on a motorcycle. There was a white light blinding me from the rider which was trying to run me off the road. I then saw a tunnel going down and people were going down the tunnel. Jesus said: *"My people, this vision is about many who are in the fast lane in life, but they are being misled by a real evil spirit. Those, who deny there are real demons, have trouble even admitting there is sin in the world. The devil wants you to believe that he and hell do not exist. If you do not believe sin is bad and keeps you from Me, then your conscience has not been properly formed on good and evil. I am loving and merciful, but sins cannot be forgiven unless you are sorry and repent for them. If you deny that you are a sinner and deny that you need Me as a Savior, then you truly will be lost. There is a hell for the unjust and they will be judged there if they refuse to accept Me. Hell was made for the defiant angels, but men, who purposely offend Me without repenting, will be condemned there if they so choose. My Word in Scripture is true and anyone, denying My Word, is not following My Will. Trust in My leading you to Me in love and continue fighting the lies of the evil one who would want you to deny My revelation to man."*

Monday, December 30, 1996:

After Communion, I could see some children of various ages. Jesus said: *"My people, I love the children and I called them to Me at all times. Remember how I asked that no one should mis-*

lead the least of My little ones lest a millstone be placed around their necks and they be thrown into the sea. All of My children are precious and they need your protection from the evils of the world. Now, even your electronic marvels are attracting innocent children to entrapments by older adults. You must watch your children closely, even from those whom you should be able to trust. Daycare providers and even teachers are abusing My little ones. Pray that their guardian angels may be attentive to their protection when they are out of your sight. I also, ask you to pray for those considering abortions, that they may not harm their babies. Killing these babies is the worst of your crimes against Me. Encourage people to treat life as precious at the early and later stages of life, especially."

Later, I could see some houses burning and they were close together in the cities. Jesus said: *"My people, I am showing the chaos in the streets and the arson which will cause many fires. Roving bands will be looting for food, fuel and valuables. When you see these things happening, know the tribulation is beginning. You will be safe for awhile, until they come searching for those believing in My Name. This age will be tried by fire and My purification must cleanse the evil that lies within each soul. Seek Me to forgive your sins and you shall be saved. Trust in My leading you to safety, and you will be protected from the evil ones. Come to My refuges and hiding places and you will find rest amidst the chaos. If you seek Me, you will save your soul, but if you seek only the pleasures of the world, your hands will be empty. Seek to do good in helping your neighbor, and your deeds will testify for you in My eyes. Do everything for Me as you follow My Will."*

Tuesday, December 31, 1996:

After Communion, I could see a huge fault widen from an earthquake. In the large crevice I could see red flowing as either lava or the water turning blood red. Jesus said: *"My people, many of My disciples thought the end was near for My Second Coming not long after My death. I did console them by telling them to live their lives as normal, but only to be always watchful. It is more important to be ready to die by having your spiritual house always in order by frequent confession. This is because you may die before I have My Second Coming. Your age has had many more signs to indicate that you are in the end times. The vision is showing you of severe earthquakes and large crevices as My Second Coming is near. The red flow represents one of the plagues you will receive as the angel will turn the rivers into blood similar to the plagues of egypt. Again, I remind you, My people, to pray and keep yourselves ready, for you know not the time nor the hour of My return."*

Later, I could see a box of cigarettes and then some candy bars. Jesus said: *"My people, many think the beginning of a new year is a time for making new resolutions to improve their life, but usually in a secular manner. It would be wonderful if people would think about resolving to live better lives in their faith. Now would be a great time to improve your spiritual habits. When you work to make your life more pleasing to Me, you are making progress toward your perfection. As with most resolutions though, you have to work extra hard to make your resolution stick throughout the whole year. You will be more successful, if you make your change an intimate part of your life. When something you do is a part of you, you do it automatically without having to remember it all the time. Once something becomes second nature to you, then you may be ready to advance even further in your improvements. I love you, My people, and I am giving you some suggestions how best to improve your spiritual lives. Remember in all that you do, that you do it to follow My Will. This is your guideline to see if something is worthy to please Me, that you test the spirit if it is according to My Will. Pray for discernment from the Holy Spirit if you truly have trouble determining My Will."*

Prepare for the Great Tribulation and the Era of Peace

Index

hiding, Antichrist (Jesus) 11/17/96
martryed or protected (Jesus) 10/29/96
Divine Will
live His Will every moment (Jesus) 11/10/96
submit, narrow gate (Jesus) 10/31/96
end times
prepare, love God, neighbor (Jesus) 11/10/96
Era of Peace
animals, aging process (Jesus) 10/6/96
harmony of animals, Noah (Jesus) 11/7/96
purification to come fast (Jesus) 11/7/96
rejuvenated bodies (Jesus) 10/7/96
evangelization
grace of mission, shrine
(Mother Cabrini) 11/17/96
personal mission (Jesus) 10/19/96
preach gospel message (Holy Spirit) 10/28/96
events
speeded up (Jesus) 11/25/96
evil age
injustices, final years (Jesus) 10/21/96
faith
practice by example (Jesus) 10/12/96
take off masks of world (Jesus) 10/31/96
family
sacredness of life (Jesus) 11/18/96
famine
manna provided (Jesus) 10/17/96
prepare food prudently (Jesus) 10/10/96
prepare for shortages (Jesus) 11/14/96
some critical of message (Jesus) 10/31/96
famine and food
no hoarding (Jesus) 10/3/96
fires
wealth taken away (Jesus) 10/23/96
first, second Resurrection
first, second deaths (Jesus) 11/29/96
glasses to see in dark
spying electrical devices (Jesus) 10/3/96
Guardian Angels
protect you from evil
(Angel Mark) 10/2/96

harvest
farmers move to new land (Jesus) 10/24/96
harvest of souls
prepare for purification (Jesus) 10/3/96
harvesting souls
convert to dying day (Jesus) 10/20/96
healings
miraculously answered (Jesus) 12/1/96
spiritual first/God's Will (Jesus) 10/8/96
hearts
ice cold, melt with love (Jesus) 11/8/96
helicopters
investigating people (Jesus) 11/14/96
helicopters & satellites
means of searching (Jesus) 10/29/96
hiding
refuges and angels (Jesus) 10/17/96
tunnels, angels to lead (Jesus) 11/24/96
Holy Lands
pray for peace (Jesus) 10/10/96
Holy Rosary feast
pray family rosary (Mary) 10/3/96
homeless
relatives, less fortunate (Jesus) 11/21/96
hope
in adversity (Jesus) 10/25/96
hospitality
to neighbor, love for God (Jesus) 10/8/96
humble
meek inherit the earth (Jesus) 11/25/96
identification
Christian for death camps (Jesus) 10/22/96
image of Jesus
focus on Him, one Body (Jesus) 10/5/96
imposter pope
will promote Antichrist (Jesus) 10/15/96
Jonah
warning of purification (Jesus) 11/18/96
judgment
forgiveness, prodigal son (Jesus) 11/12/96
prepare soul in confession (Jesus) 12/5/96

schism

   modernism vs remnant (Jesus)   10/5/96

Scripture

   read each day (Jesus)   11/14/96

Second Coming

   convert, prepare (Jesus)   11/9/96

   signs of the end times (Jesus)   11/26/96

sin

   confession, forgiveness (Jesus)   11/20/96

singing

   praises, joy & love (Jesus)   10/10/96

sins

   scorching the earth (Jesus)   10/24/96

soul

   beauty in eyes, forgive (Jesus)   11/10/96

souls

   parched, heal soul first (Jesus)   11/21/96

St. Therese

   call on her for help (St. Therese)   10/1/96

stock market crash

   One World Government (Jesus)   11/19/96

suffering

   offer up each day (Jesus)   11/25/96

   price for souls (Jesus)   12/4/96

   test of endurance (Jesus)   11/16/96

   understanding of suffering (Jesus)   12/3/96

suffering, window of

   do not question God (Jesus)   10/4/96

terrorism

   TWA 800 flight/Olympics (Jesus)   10/11/96

testing & hardships

   snow removal, spiritual life (Jesus)   11/27/96

Thanksgiving

   foodshelves, make amend (Jesus)   11/14/96

   we are blessed with gifts (Jesus)   11/28/96

time

   events speeding up (Jesus)   10/25/96

time

   will speed up (Jesus)   11/21/96

trains to detention center

   enemies of Antichrist (Jesus)   10/3/96

tribulation

   government taken over (Jesus)   10/10/96

   know meaning of Word (Jesus)   11/3/96

triumph

   conquer evil (Jesus)   10/11/96

United States

   hand out, greed for power (Jesus)   10/19/96

   rejects blessings, perish (Jesus)   10/24/96

warning

   football field, repent (Jesus)   10/25/96

   prepare with confession (Jesus)   10/13/96

weather

   snow and fires (Jesus)   11/2/96

wise virgins

   prepare for His Coming (Jesus)   10/29/96

work

   means of salvation (Jesus)   10/9/96

Prepare for the Great Tribulation and the Era of Peace

More Messages from God through John Leary

If you would like to take advantage of more precious words from Jesus and Mary and apply them to your lives, read the first three volumes of messages and visions given to us through John s special gift. Each book contains a full year of daily messages and visions. As Jesus and Mary said in volume IV:

Hear my messages and read again the old messages that you may realize these words of warning and preparation are for your age at this time. Mary 6/24/96

...there will come a time when you will be banned from speaking and you will rely on your books to spread the message. Jesus 6/26/96

Listen to my words of warning, and you will be ready to share in the beauty of the second coming. Jesus 7/4/96

I will work miracles of conversion on those who read these books with an open mind. Jesus 9/5/96

Prepare for the Great Tribulation and the Era of Peace

Volume I - *Messages received from July 1993 to June 1994*
ISBN# 1-882972-69-4 . . . . 256pp. - $7.95

Volume II - *Messages received from July 1994 to June 1995*
ISBN# 1-882972-72-4 . . . . 352pp. - $8.95

Volume III - *Messages received from July 1995 to July 10, 1996*
ISBN# 1-882972-77-5 . . . . 384pp. - $8.95

Volume IV - *Messages received from July 11, 1996 to Sep. 30, 1996*
ISBN# 1-882972-91-0 . . . . 104pp. - $2.95

Visit your local bookstore for other great titles from:

QUEENSHIP PUBLISHING

Do Whatever Love Requires - *Carol Ameche & Harriet Hammons*
ISBN# 1-882972-61-1 . . . . $2.95

For the Soul of the Family - *Thomas W. Petrisko*
The story of the apparitions of the Virgin Mary to Estela Ruiz
and how one family came back to God.
ISBN# 1-882972-90-2 . . . . $9.95

Call of the Ages - *Thomas W. Petrisko*
The Apparitions and Revelations of the Virgin Mary
Fortell the Coming Fall of Evil and an Era of Peace
ISBN# 1-882972-59-7 . . . . $11.95

Trial, Tribulation and Triumph - *Desmond A. Birch*
Before, During and After Antichrist
ISBN #1-882972-73-2 . . . . $19.50

Mary: God s Supreme Masterpiece - *Fr. Bartholomew Gottemoller*
ISBN# 1-882972-48-1 . . . . $5.95

Jesus, Peter and the Keys - *Scott Butler, Norman Dahlgren, David Hess*
A Scriptural Handbook on the Papacy
ISBN# 1-882972-54-6 . . . . $14.95

The Gift of the Church - *by Monsignor Bob Guste*
Current Questions and Objections about the Catholic Church and
Down-to-Earth Answers
ISBN# 1-882972-01-5 . . . . $7.95

The Coming Chastisement - *Br. Craig Driscoll*
ISBN #1-882972-41-X $1.95

The Light of Love - *Patricia Devlin*
My Angel Shall Go Before Me
ISBN #1-882972-53-8 . . . . $8.75

Marian Apparitions Today - *Fr. Edward D. O'Connor*
Why So Many?
ISBN #1-882972-71-6 . . . . $7.95